SO-CDC-504

THE MATTHEAN REDACTION
OF A PRIMITIVE APOSTOLIC COMMISSIONING:
AN EXEGESIS OF MATTHEW 28:16-20

WITHDRAWN

WITHDRAWN

BS
2575.2
.H82
1974

THE MATTHEAN REDACTION OF A PRIMITIVE APOSTOLIC COMMISSIONING:

AN EXEGESIS OF MATTHEW 28:16-20

by

Benjamin Jerome Hubbard

Published by

SOCIETY OF BIBLICAL LITERATURE

and

SCHOLARS' PRESS

DISSERTATION SERIES, NUMBER 19

1974

HIEBERT LIBRARY
PACIFIC COLLEGE · M. B. SEMINARY
FRESNO, CALIF. 93702

12660

THE MATTHEAN REDACTION OF A PRIMITIVE APOSTOLIC COMMISSIONING:

AN EXEGESIS OF MATTHEW 28:16-20

by

Benjamin Jerome Hubbard
Department of Religious Studies
St. Jerome's College
Waterloo, Ontario
Canada

Ph.D., 1973
Graduate College of
University of Iowa

Advisor:
George W. Nickelsburg

Copyright © 1974

by

The Society of Biblical Literature

Library of Congress Catalog Card Number: 74:16566
ISBN: 0-88414-047-4

Printed in the United States of America

Printing Department
University of Montana
Missoula, Montana 59801

TABLE OF CONTENTS

ABBREVIATIONS

ASTI	Annual of the Swedish Theological Institute
B Res	Biblical Research
Bl.-Debr.	F. Blass and A. Debrunner, A Greek Grammar of the New Testament and Other Early Christian Literature (trans. and rev. by R. Funk). Chicago, 1964.
Ev Th	Evangelische Theologie
HB	The Hebrew Bible
HST	R. Bultmann, The History of the Synoptic Tradition. ET: Oxford, 1963.
HTR	Harvard Theological Review
IB	The Interpreter's Bible, ed. by G. A. Buttrick. 12 Vols. New York, 1952.
JBC	The Jerome Biblical Commentary, ed. by R. Brown, J. Fitzmeyer, and R. Murphy. 2 Vols. Englewood Cliffs, N.J.; 1968.
JBL	Journal of Biblical Literature
LXX	The Septuagint (Greek) version of the Hebrew Bible
MT	The Masoretic Text of the Hebrew Bible
NTS	New Testament Studies
PCB	Peake's Commentary on the Bible, ed. by M. Black and H. H. Rowley. London, 1962.
PG	Patrologiae cursus completus Series Graeca, ed. by J. P. Migne. Paris, 1875-87.
TDNT	Theological Dictionary of the New Testament, ed. by G. Kittel. 8 Vols. in English to date (A-Y). Grand Rapids, Mich.; 1964-
Theol Z	Theologische Zeitschrift
TIM	G. Bornkamm, G. Barth, H. J. Held, Tradition and Interpretation in Matthew. ET: Philadelphia, 1963.
ZAW	Zeitschrift für die alttestamentliche Wissenschaft
ZNW	Zeitschrift für die neutestamentliche Wissenschaft
Z Th K	Zeitschrift für Theologie und Kirche

ACKNOWLEDGMENTS

I wish to express special thanks to my thesis supervisor,
Dr. George W. Nickelsburg of the School of Religion, for his guidance
in the writing of this thesis. I also wish to thank the other members
of my thesis committee from the School of Religion, all of whom assisted
me in my work: Drs. Helen Goldstein, J. Kenneth Kuntz and James F.
McCue.

I am indebted to my colleague at St. Jerome's College, Waterloo,
Ontario, Dr. Michael Coogan, who assisted me in various ways, particularly
by checking all of the Hebrew transliterations.

Jean Spowart of Kitchener, Ontario typed the thesis. She
deserves my gratitude for her painstaking efforts.

To my wife, Judith, tôdāh rabbāh for her preparation of the
Bibliography and for her patience and inspiration.

ABSTRACT

There is no scholarly consensus regarding the literary form of
Mt. 28:16-20, Jesus' Easter commission of his disciples. A survey of the
narratives of the commissionings of patriarchs and prophets in the Hebrew
Bible, however, indicates a recurring form: circumstantial introduction, confrontation between commissioner (usually God) and one to be commissioned,
reaction to presence of deity (sometimes), commission proper, protest to task
outlined in commission (sometimes), word of reassurance from deity, conclusion.

When applied to Mt. 28:16-20, the following elements can be isolated:
introduction, confrontation, reaction, commission and reassurance. Also the
passage contains language characteristic of Hebrew Bible commissions and
recapitulates major themes in Matthew.

The Matthean commission and the parallel material in Jn. 20:19-23
and Lk. 24:36-53 yields a primitive apostolic commissioning underlying all
three: "Jesus appeared to the eleven. When they saw him they were glad,
though some disbelieved. Then he said: 'Preach (the gospel) to all nations,
(Baptize) in my name for the forgiveness of sins. (And behold,) I will send
the Holy Spirit upon you.'" The proto-commission was one step removed from
the actual account of Jesus' Easter commission on the lips of an original
disciple. Spoken by an early Christian missionary, it added the stress on the
Gentile mission.

Matthew has taken the proto-commission and redacted it to give it a
closer correspondence to the form and language of a Hebrew Bible commission.

The Markan version of the Easter Commission (Mk. 16:14-20) originated
with someone other than the author of the Gospel proper and was derived principally from material in Matthew, Luke and John. However, vv. 15f. (the
commission proper) may contain material from an independent tradition ultimately stemming from the proto-commission.

PREFACE

One major study has appeared since the completion of this dissertation which lends support to its basic viewpoint. Referring to Mt. 28:16-20,
Ellis in <u>Matthew: His Mind and His Message</u> (Collegeville, Minn., 1974) states:
"Jesus commissions his Apostles, as Yahweh had commissioned his prophets..."
(p. 23; see pp. 22 and 24).

With respect to the form critical analysis of Hebrew Bible commissioning accounts in Chapter 2 of the present work, one additional study should
be mentioned: Burke O. Long, "Prophetic Call Traditions and Reports of
Visions," <u>ZAW</u> 84 (1972), 494-500. He is in substantial agreement with the
conclusions drawn in that Chapter, though the scope of his article is somewhat different.

Waterloo, Ontario
July, 1974

Chapter One THE PROBLEM

I. Introduction

The last five verses of the Gospel according to Matthew read

as follows:

> (28:16) Now the eleven disciples went to Galilee, to
> the mountain to which Jesus had directed them.
> (17) And when they saw him they worshiped him;
> but some doubted. (18) And Jesus came and
> said to them, "All authority in heaven and on
> earth has been given to me. (19) Go therefore
> and make disciples of all nations, baptizing
> them in the name of the Father and of the Son
> and of the Holy Spirit, (20) teaching them to
> observe all that I have commanded you; and lo,
> I am with you always, to the close of the age.[1]

These verses have always been considered important because of

the light they shed on the nature of the Christian missionary endeavor.[2]

In modern scholarship they have been seen by several exegetes as "the

key to an understanding of the entire book [Matthew's]."[3] Although the

pericope has been the subject of many enlightening contemporary studies,

one problem in particular has remained unsolved: the literary form or

structure of the passage. Trilling summed up the situation by saying:

---

[1] Unless otherwise stated, all scriptural quotations are from the Revised
Standard Version.

[2] S. Johnson, "Matthew, Exegesis," IB 7, 620.

[3] O. Michel, "Der Abschluss des Matthäus-Evangeliums," Ev Th 10 (1950-51),
21. Cp. E. P. Blair, Jesus in the Gospel of Matthew (New York, 1960),
pp. 45f.; W. Trilling, Das Wahre Israel (Munich, 1964³), p. 21.

"A determination of the form critical problem has not yet been satis-
factorily made."[1] The immediate aim of this study is to seek an answer
to the problem. The long range aim is to determine what material Matthew
had at hand when he composed 28:16-20 and how he redacted it to its present shape. Our hope is that, in answering these interrelated questions,
some additional light will be shed on Matthew's closing verses and on
his Gospel as a whole.

II. The Discussion

A number of scholars in this century have proposed solutions
to the problem of the literary form of 28:16(18)[2]-20. We will review
and evaluate each of these and thereby prepare the way for a considera-
tion of our own solution.

A. Martin Dibelius

M. Dibelius discusses 28:16-20 in connection with mythology.[3]
He describes a myth as a story which in some way tells of the many-sided
activities of the gods, e.g., by relating a religious rite to its original form in the career of a particular deity.[4] Although 28:16-20 does
not as such constitute a myth (as does, e.g., the Baptism of Jesus,

---

[1]Trilling, p. 49.

[2]Most of them focus only on the actual words of commissioning (vv. 18b-20)
rather than on the entire pericope. We consider this a mistake since vv.
16f. are integrally related to the words of commissioning. More will be
said on the matter in the discussion of the proposed solutions.

[3]In Die Formgeschichte des Evangeliums (Tübingen, 1961[4]).

[4]Ibid., p. 265.

Mk. 1:9-11 par.), a "mythical attitude" can be traced therein. Dibelius

does this by comparing the pericope to Mt. 11:25-30 which contains words

of Jesus differing sharply from the typical Synoptic style. He notes,

in particular, the combination of self-recommendation ("all things have

been delivered to me by my Father . . .") and the preaching of conver-

sion ("come to me, all who labor . . . Take my yoke upon you, and learn

from me . . ."). Such a combination is "the typical mark of the divine

or semi-divine herald of a revelation in Hellenistic religiousness,

i.e.,of a mythological person."[1] The same combination is found, he

believes, in the Matthean commission: "All authority in heaven and on

earth has been given to me. Go therefore and make disciples . . .

baptizing them . . . teaching them to observe all that I have commanded

you . . ." Moreover, the dignity of the risen Lord is expressed more

fully here than in 11:25ff.: he has been given all authority (28:18b)

and his disciples are assured of his enduring presence until the end of

the world (28:20b). Thus the "mythological character" of the pericope

is more unmistakeable than in Mt. 11.[2] Finally, Dibelius notes that the

words of commissioning in vv. 18-20 stand in no historical situation

since all the questions raised by the narrative of vv. 16f. remain un-

answered: How does Jesus appear and disappear? How are the doubters

dealt with? Which mountain is meant? The lack of a historical setting

---

[1]Dibelius, p. 282.

[2]Ibid., p. 285.

4

for the commission adds to the mythical attitude of the pericope.[1] What
we have, then, in 28:16-20 is a word of revelation from a divine figure
(the risen Jesus) set in a mythological framework.

We would question Dibelius' exclusive concentration on the
similarities between Mt. 11:25-30 and 28:16-20. The principal likeness
is between 11:27 ("All things have been delivered to me by Father . . .")
and 28:18b ("All authority . . . given to me"). Yet there is nothing in
11:25-30 about Jesus' followers being given a universal mission to make
disciples and to teach them the observance of all his commands, as in
28:16-20.

We also wonder why Dibelius has not at least considered the
possibility that the Hebrew Bible[2] might have influenced the composition
of Matthew's concluding verses. Expressions such as "make disciples of
all nations" and "I am with you always, to the close of the age" have a
Biblical rather than a Hellenistic ring. In short we feel that Dibelius
has too readily assigned 28:16-20 to the domain of the mythological.

B. Rudolf Bultmann

R. Bultmann describes 28:16-20 as "a sort of cult legend in
virtue of the appended instruction to baptize."[3] He defines "legends" as
"those parts of the tradition which are not miracle stories in the proper
sense, but which instead of being historical in character are religious

---

[1]Dibelius, Ibid.

[2]Hereafter abbreviated HB.

[3]HST, p. 286.

and edifying."[1] He compares 28:16-20 as a cult legend to the Markan

Last Supper account (14:22-25) and to the story of Jesus' baptism (Mk.

1:9-11 par.).[2] Each of these pericopes attained its present form in a

cultic setting. In the case of 28:16-20, a loose tradition of a mis-

sionary charge has been finally fixed by means of the Church's cult.

Looked at from the other side, the ordinance to baptize has been "appended"

to the missionary charge.

Our basic difficulty with Bultmann's viewpoint is that he does

not adequately explain the overall shape of the pericope, but simply

characterizes it as a "cult legend." This does not do justice to the

elements contained therein, e.g., Jesus' statement of authority (v. 18b)

or his promise to remain always with the disciples (v. 20b).

C. Georg Strecker

G. Strecker considers 28:18-20 to be the combination of a pre-

Matthean "word of revelation" with a Matthean expansion bringing the

passage into harmony with his theological position.[3] The word of reve-

lation consists of three parts which speak about:

    (1) the authority of the exalted one (18b);

    (2) his command to baptize (19b);

    (3) his promise to remain with his disciples (20b).[4]

---

[1] Ibid., p. 244.

[2] Ibid., pp. 305f.

[3] Der Weg der Gerechtigkeit (Göttingen, 1962), p. 210.

[4] Ibid.

Vv. 18a and 20a contain typically Matthean language[1]; and v. 19a the universal missionary command which is a major redactional element in the First Gospel.[2] The Sitz im Leben of the pre-Matthean word of revelation was the liturgical tradition of the Matthean community. Central to Strecker's analysis is his contention that the baptismal command was part of the tradition which Matthew inherited.[3] It is not Matthean in language, and the redactor would hardly have introduced the practice into his community.[4]

The strength of his position lies in his contention that traditional and redactional elements have gone into the makeup of 28:16-20, and that Matthew did not himself compose the triadic baptismal command. The weakness lies in the preponderance attributed to the baptismal command. The tradition known to the redactor would be saying roughly the following: "All authority in heaven and on earth has been given to me. Baptize in the name of the Father and of the Son and of the Holy Spirit. I am with you always." We would question the existence of a tradition

---

[1]Specifically: προσελθὼν, ἐλάλησεν αὐτοῖς λέγων (18a); τηρεῖν, πάντα, ἐνετειλάμην, καὶ ἰδοὺ, συντελείας τοῦ αἰῶνος (20a). Ibid., p. 209.

[2]Ibid. He lists πορεύεσθαι, οὖν and μαθητεύειν as redactional words in 19a.

[3]He also expresses this opinion in "The Concept of History in Matthew," Journal of the American Academy of Religion 35 (March, 1967), p. 229: "In the redactional context, Matthew has not attempted to establish baptism as a sacramental occurrence, nor does the baptismal formula quoted in triad form on 28:19 have any support in the redactional material."

[4]Strecker, Weg, p. 209.

in which a declaration of universal authority and a promise of the abiding presence of Jesus support simply a command to baptize.

D. Otto Michel and Joachim Jeremias

Both O. Michel and, under his influence, J. Jeremias attempt to explain Mt. 28:18-20 as an enthronement hymn.[1] The Matthean tradition ✓ viewed the well-known Son of Man enthronement scene in Dan. 7:13-14 as fulfilled through Easter.[2] Thus the pericope is both linguistically and form critically a christological reshaping of the words in Daniel. The LXX of Dan. 7:14 which is translated here is particularly significant:

> And he was given (ἐδόθη, as in 28:18) authority
> (ἐξουσία, v. 18) and all nations (πάντα
> τὰ ἔθνη, v. 19) of the earth (τῆς γῆς, v. 18)
> race by race and all glory were in his service. And
> his authority (ἐξουσία, v. 18) is an everlasting
> authority which may not be taken away, his kingdom
> also one which may not be destroyed.[3]

Form critically Dan. 7:13-14, Mt. 28:18-20 and Phil. 2:9-11 are triple-action coronation texts. In each there is an intimate relationship between three elements: (1) authority (2) lordship and (3) the recognition by all people of the bestowal of these qualities.[4]

---

[1] Michel, "Der Abschluss der Matthäusevangeliums," Ev Th 10 (1950) 22f.; Jeremias, Jesus' Promise to the Nations (Naperville, Ill.; 1958), pp. 38f.

[2] Michel, p. 22.

[3] Translation mine. Theodotion's Greek version of Dan. 7:14 differs from the LXX in some words (it is closer to the MT), but the same form critical pattern is maintained.

[4] Michel, p. 22.

Jeremias develops the parallels to the triple-action coronation texts even further and cites two other NT examples of the form:
1 Tim. 3:16 and Heb. 1:5-14. The Egyptian coronation ritual, he explains,
consisted of the following three actions: 1. Elevation; 2. Presentation
or Proclamation; 3. Enthronement of the new king.[1] As applied to the
four NT texts just mentioned the threefold (Christological) enthronement
pattern can be recognized in each as follows:[2]

> Phil. 2:9-11 (1. Elevation or Exaltation, v. 9a;
> 2. Proclamation of the name above every name, v. 9b;
> 3. homage to the Enthroned one by gesture and con-
> fession, vv. 10f.)
>
> 1 Tim. 3:16 (1. the Justification by resurrection
> [i.e., the Elevation] of the one manifested on
> earth; 2. the Announcement of this to heaven and
> earth; 3. his Assumption of the kingdom on earth and
> in heaven.)
>
> Heb. 1:5-14 (1. Elevation as Son of God, vv. 5f.;
> 2. Proclamation of his eternal Kingship, vv. 7-12;
> 3. Enthronement, vv. 13f.)
>
> Mt. 28:18-20 (1. Assumption of all power by the risen
> Christ, v. 18; 2. the injunction to Proclaim his
> authority among all nations, vv. 19f.; 3. the word of
> Power, v. 20b.)[3]

It is hard for us to deny that the wording of Dan. 7:14 (LXX)
is echoed in the Matthean pericope.[4] Nor would we deny that Phil. 2:9-11,

---

[1] Jeremias, p. 38. He provides no sources for his knowledge of this
ritual. See H. Frankfort, Kingship and the Gods (Chicago, 1948), pp.
105f.; J. Kaster, The Literature and Mythology of Ancient Egypt (London,
1968), pp. 121ff.

[2] Ibid., pp. 38f.

[3] By protecting his messengers, the Son of Man displays his royal power;
cp. Lk. 10:19, Mk. 16:17-18 (Jeremias, p. 39).

[4] We intend to make clear the implications of this allusion to Dan. 7:14
in Chapter Three. For the moment, my concern is simply to show that the
allusion does not clinch the enthronement-hymn theory for Michel and Jeremias.

1 Tim. 3:16 and Heb. 1:5-14 are Christological hymns in which the exaltation of Jesus is described in successive steps.

However, there are a number of difficulties involved in viewing Mt. 28:18-20 as another example of an enthronement hymn. Unlike the genuine hymns we have just examined, the Matthean verses deal primarily with the command of the exalted Christ, not with his person.[1] Whereas in 1 Tim., Phil. 2 and -- less clearly -- Heb. 1, his career is described in successive steps, Mt. 28 relates only the fact that he has been granted universal authority (18b). The direction which the Matthean passage takes in vv. 19f. is towards making disciples for the exalted Jesus rather than the exaltation itself. Furthermore, 1 Tim., Phil. 2 and Heb. 1 (as schematized above by Jeremias) stress the way in which the Christian community sings the hymn of enthronement and thus proclaims the greatness of the Christ. In Mt. 28 it is the exalted Lord himself (first person) who speaks rather than the grateful community.[2] Finally, Jeremias' schematization of Mt. 28:18-20 (see above) does not correspond closely enough with the facts. Jesus does not assume all authority in the final scene of Matthew's Gospel (so, Jeremias) but already possesses it. Nor does he command that his authority as such be proclaimed (Jeremias), but that disciples be made, baptized and instructed. Nor, lastly, is he stating a word of power about himself in 28:20b (Jeremias) but a word of reassurance to his disciples.

---

[1] Trilling, p. 46.

[2] Cf. Strecker, _Weg_, p. 210, n. 3.

E. Ferdinand Hahn

F. Hahn[1] accepts a modified version of the enthronement pattern (which he considers to be most completely expressed in Phil. 2:9-11). This pattern is suggested by 28:18b where the granting of complete authority to Jesus is joined to his "lordship over heaven and earth -- that is, with the idea of exaltation."[2] However, Hahn points out that the words about authority in 18b do not directly speak of the act of enthronement but are a revelation of the exaltation already accomplished. The theme of the exercise of sovereignty by the exalted Lord is expressed in 20b where his perpetual presence and support are expressed. He does not consider Dan. 7:14 to be primary HB point of reference in 28:18-20, but rather LXX Ps. 109:1 (= 110:1 in MT). Here, and throughout the Psalm, the enthronement theme occurs repeatedly and holds out the promise of the final lordship of the Messiah over the powers of the world (LXX Ps. 109:5-6).[3] In Mt. 28:18-20 "Hellenist Jewish Christianity" replaced this HB theme of the subjection of the "nations" (= ἔθνεσιν in LXX Ps. 109:6) by that of the gospel to the Gentiles in the last days. In this context baptism (28:19) signifies the ongoing activity of the exalted one who, even in the present, bestows salvation on those accepting the gospel. Hahn does admit that vv. 19f. reflect the "editorial intervention" of

---

[1] *Mission in the New Testament* (ET: Naperville, Ill.; 1965).

[2] *Ibid.*, p. 66.

[3] *Ibid.*, pp. 66f. Hahn notes that in the prototypical enthronement hymn, Phil. 2:9-11, Jesus is called κύριος (v. 11), a key word in LXX Ps. 109:1.

Matthew (e.g., the "triadic baptismal formula" and the Matthean term
μαθητεύειν, "make disciples").[1]

The main weakness of Hahn's approach is his failure to stress
the missionary command sufficiently. E.g., Jesus' promise of his abiding presence (v. 20b) is not tied to the idea of his exercise of sovereignty as much as to that of his support of those who have gone to make
all nations his disciples. Furthermore, his view that Ps. 109 (LXX) is
the primary biblical point of reference for 28:18-20 rests on the assumption that these verses, like the Psalm, have an enthronement motif.
However as we tried to show in the case of Michel and Jeremias, this
remains questionable. Since it does, the heavy reliance on Ps. 109 (LXX)
does not appear justifiable. Moreover, the theme of an actual mission
to the Gentiles occurs most notably elsewhere in the HB, especially in
Is. 49:6 and Jer. 1:5.[2]

F. C. H. Dodd

C. H. Dodd approaches the problem by dividing every resurrection narrative in the four Gospels into one of two categories: "tales"
and "concise narratives".[3] The stories of the walk to Emmaus (Lk.
24:13-35) and of the meal by the Sea of Galilee (Jn. 21:1-14) are clear

---

[1] Ibid., p. 67.

[2] Cf. Is. 2:2-4.

[3] "The Appearances of the Risen Christ: An Essay in Form-Criticism of
the Gospels" in Studies in the Gospels (ed. D. E. Nineham)(Oxford, 1957),
pp. 9f. These are the two main categories of all Gospel narratives,
according to Dodd.

examples of tales. The best examples of concise narratives are Mt.
28:8-10, 16-20 and Jn. 20:19-21. Dodd finds a common pattern in these
three pericopes consisting of the following five elements:

    1. The situation: Jesus' followers bereft of their Lord.

    2. The appearance of the Lord.

    3. The greeting.

    4. The recognition.

    5. The word of command.

Using these index numbers to compare the three passages in question, we
get the following scheme:

Mt. 28:8-10	Mt. 28:16-20	Jn. 20:19-21
1. Women were on way from tomb to disciples.	Eleven disciples went to Galilee to mountain appointed for rendezvous.	Disciples gathered on Sunday evening with closed doors (for fear of Jews).
2. Jesus met them.	Jesus approached.	Jesus stood in their midst.
3. He said χαίρετε.[1]	------------------	He said εἰρήνη ὑμῖν.
4. They approached, grasped his feet, worshipped him.	Seeing Jesus, they worshipped him but some doubted.	Disciples were glad when they saw the Lord.
5. Go and tell my brethren to go to Galilee where they will see me.	Go and make disciples of all nations . . .	As the Father has sent me, so I send you.

    Dodd also notes that there is an element of doubt or fear in
all three of the narratives. It is explicit in Mt. 28:17: "but some

---

[1]Dodd notes (p. 11) that χαίρετε is the normal Greek greeting and
εἰρήνη ὑμῖν a Greek translation of the normal Hebrew or Aramaic
greeting (on the assumption that an Aramaic tradition underlay Jn. 20:
19-21).

doubted;" implied in the "fear not" of Mt. 28:10; and implied in Jesus'
showing of his hands and side in Jn. 20:20.[1] Furthermore, all three
work up ("like the 'Paradigms' or 'Pronouncement-stories'") to an important saying of Jesus.

Dodd sheds considerable light on 28:16-20 because he deals
with the entire pericope and not just the words of commissioning (18b-
20). His schematization of the formal elements is accurate for the most
part. He may, however, have put too much stress on the "Greeting". It
is absent from 28:16-20 and from Mk. 16:14-15 (which he also classifies
as a concise narrative.)[2] We also think that Dodd has not sufficiently
enough accounted for two important aspects of 28:16-20: the declaration
of authority (18b) and the promise of abiding presence (20b).

We now turn to a series of four studies in which a model for
the structure of 28:16(18)-20 is sought from the HB.

G. Johannes Munck

J. Munck[3] brings to light the existence of several farewell
speeches in the HB and in post-biblical Jewish literature. The best HB

---

[1]Ibid., p. 12. In the two Matthean pericopes the doubt is overcome not
by an explicit tender of proof (as in Jn. 20:20), but by the women's
touching of Jesus' feet (thus assuring themselves that they are confront-
ing a real person) in 28:9, and by Jesus' statement that he possesses
universal authority in 28:18.

[2]He contends that Jesus' reproach of the disciples for their incredulity
has "replaced" the Greeting (p. 16). This is unconvincing because Jesus'
reproach is narrated in the third person and there is no direct quotation
as in the Greetings in Mt. 28:9 and Jn. 20:19.

[3]"Discours d'adieu dans le Nouveau Testament et dans la littérature
biblique" in Aux Sources de la Tradition Chrétienne, Mélanges Goguel
(Paris, 1950), pp. 155-70.

example is Jacob's speech to his sons (Gen. 47:29-50:14). After obtaining assurance that Joseph will bury him with his forefathers (47:29-31), Jacob falls ill and blesses Joseph and his sons (Ch. 48). He also recalls the key events in his life (48:3-7). Then he gathers his sons and announces what will befall them in the "days to come" (49:1-27). He blesses them, charges them all to bury him with his fathers and dies (49:28-33). Finally, Jacob is embalmed and taken to Canaan for burial (50:1-14).[1]

Munck finds a similar pattern in Tob. 14:3-11 where Tobit blesses his son and grandsons, predicts what will befall them and exhorts them to keep the Law.[2]

The best NT example of the farewell speech form is Paul's address to the elders of the Church at Ephesus (Acts 20:17-38). It has the following pattern:

(1) "Before his departure for martyrdom,"[3] Paul assembles the elders to address them for the last time with his final instructions.

(2) He makes the fact of his departure clear.

(3) He presents himself as a model to imitate in serving the community.

---

[1] Ibid., pp. 155f. Munck sees a similar pattern present in the Book of Deuteronomy (Moses' farewell speech), in Jos. 23-24 (Joshua's) and in 1 Kg. 2:1-9 (David's).

[2] Munck, p. 157. Other examples which he cites are: 4 Esdras 14:18ff., Baruch 76-77, Enoch 91:1-19 and The Testament of the Twelve Patriarchs.

[3] Ibid., p. 161.

(4) He predicts the persecutions which the community
will endure at the hands of false teachers.[1]

Finally, Munck turns to several of the post-resurrection pericopes in which Jesus addresses the disciples. The best example here is
Lk. 24:36-53. Jesus reminds the disciples of the words he had spoken
to them while still with them (v. 44). He then instructs them to be his
witnesses when they have received the promise of his Father (vv. 48f.).[2]
Munck also characterizes Mt. 28:19-20 (sic) as a farewell speech. "Jesus
here speaks of himself as one to whom all power has been given; consequently, he gives commandments to his disciples and blesses them."[3]

Munck's form critical judgements seem generally accurate until
he turns to the post-resurrection material, particularly Mt. 28:19f.
Jesus does not announce his departure nor actually depart. He does not
predict future difficulties nor bless the disciples. He promises, on
the contrary, to remain always with them. He does, as Munck notes, give
them commandments; but this fact alone does not seem to be sufficient
justification for placing the pericope in the genre of a farewell speech.

H. Wolfgang Trilling

Trilling, as noted on p. 1 above, thinks that the form critical question has not been adequately answered. He does, though, state
an opinion on the matter.

---

[1]Ibid. Munck finds the same general pattern in 1 Tim. 4:1ff. and 2 Tim.
3:1ff. (see pp. 162f.).

[2]Ibid., p. 165.

[3]Munck, p. 165. Other examples in this group of resurrection speeches
are: Jn. 20:19-23, 21:15-23 and Acts 1:2ff. Ibid.

Vv. 18-20 exhibit a threefold pattern of revelatory word, command and promise. They correspond, thereby, to the schema of the HB speech of God (Gottesrede).[1] The three elements of the schema do not, however, appear together in any one passage. Rather, the first and second are seen in one instance, the second and third in another. The best example of a revelatory word is the expression, "I am the LORD your God who brought you out of the land of Egypt . . ." (Ex. 20:2, Dt. 5:6). It is followed by the commandments of the decalogue (Ex. 20:3ff., Dt. 5:7ff.). Thus the command is preceded by an allusion to the lordship of Yahweh and/or his saving deeds.[2] A command can also be followed by a promise so that the second and third elements are linked.[3] In this case Yahweh assures his people that the fulfilling of his commands will bring them blessings, victory over their enemies and the greatest good, his enduring presence ("I will be with you," Dt. 31:23 and often elsewhere).

The Matthean passage shows the influence of the HB pattern just described since Jesus' authoritative command (vv. 19f.) is rooted in his lordship (v. 18b) and issues in his promise (v. 20b). The fact that many of the HB speech-of-God texts cited are from Deuteronomy is not a chance occurrence. There are "radical affinities" between it and the First Gospel.[4]

---

[1]Trilling, p. 48.

[2]Ibid. He cites the following as variations of this phenomenon: Ex. 6:29; Dt. 10:12-22, 11:1-9, 17:14ff. He also compares them to the prophetic expression, "Thus says the Lord God" (Ezek. 2:4 and elsewhere).

[3]Trilling lists these examples: Dt. 31:5-6, 7-8, 23; Jos. 1:2-7, 8-9; Jer. 1:7-8.

[4]Ibid., p. 49.

Trilling's theory is valuable because it recognizes the great influence of the HB on Matthew generally and seeks to specify that influence in 28:18-20. Furthermore, several of the passages cited by him as examples of the speech-of-God schema involve the commissioning of an individual in Yahweh's service (Moses, Ex. 6:20; Joshua, Dt. 31:23, Jos. 1:2-9; Jeremiah, Jer. 1:7-8; Ezekiel, Ez. 2:4). Yet Trilling is unable to cite a single HB example wherein all three elements isolated by him occur together. Nevertheless, he has, for the first time in the studies thus far examined, introduced the possibility that the narratives of the commissionings of prophetic figures such as Joshua or Jeremiah may be related to the Matthean post-resurrection commissioning.

I. Ernst Lohmeyer

E. Lohmeyer's[1] analysis resembles that of Trilling. He speaks of a "fixed schema" in vv. 18-20: 1. self revelation, 2. commission and 3. promise.[2] Passages such as Dt. 6:4-5 are the HB counterpart of the first two elements, while commissions or commands are often followed by the promise of divine assistance. Yet Lohmeyer, like Trilling, does not provide a single example in which the three elements are actually found together.

J. Bruce Malina

B. Malina considers the model for 28:16-20 to be that of an "official decree (of the biblical type at the close of 2 Chron.)" which

---

[1] Das Evangelium des Matthäus (Göttingen, 1956).

[2] Ibid., p. 416.

also has "the overtones of a proof pattern" further nuancing the quality
and scope of the decree.[1] The specific text which exercised primary influence in Matthew was 2 Chron. 36:23 (= Ezr. 1:1-3a). This pericope is
itself a variant of the basic HB message form clearly exemplified in
Gen. 45:9-11; Num. 22:5f., 15-17.[2] Two reasons are presented for the
appeal to 2 Chron. 36. (1) There are parallels in literary form between
it and Mt. 28:18-20. (2) Just as Mt. 28:18-20 closes the Gospel, so
2 Chron. 36:23 closes the Jewish scriptures (see MT).[3] An analysis of
the decree in 2 Chron. results in the following outline of its parts:

    1. Message formula: "Thus says Cyrus king of Persia,

    2. Narration:

        (a) Statement of authority: 'The Lord, the God of
            heaven, has given me all the kingdoms of the
            earth,

        (b) Reason for command: . . . and he has charged
            me to build him a house at Jerusalem which is
            in Judah.

    3. Command:

        (a) Those commanded: Whoever is among you of all
            his people,

        (b) Motivation: may the Lord his God be with him.

        (c) Command proper: Let him go up.'"

---

[1] "The Literary Structure and Form of Mt. 28:16-20," NTS 17 (1970), 96.

[2] Ibid., 92f.

[3] Ibid., 96 (esp. n. 1).

Before going on to apply the form to Mt. 28, Malina attempts to deal
with the "puzzling" words, "but some doubted" in 28:17b. He notes that
the expression καὶ ἰδοὺ ("and lo"), when followed by a finite verb,
is often employed by Matthew to introduce something of importance.[1] In
v. 20b καὶ ἰδοὺ is followed by, "I am with you always to the close
of the age." It serves to overcome the doubt in a way that shades off
the official decree pattern into a proof pattern. The literary form of
the proof pattern consists of:

1. Prophetic Message Formula: Thus says Yahweh.

2. Motivation: I have seen, etc.

3. Announcement of Salvation: I shall give into
   your hands, etc.

4. Proof Formula: And you shall know that I am
   Yahweh.

As applied to Mt. 28:18-20, v. 18a ("and Jesus came and said to them
. . .") would correspond to no. 1 above. No. 2 is lacking; no. 3 corresponds to v. 18b ("All authority . . . to me") except that in 18b the salvation is already accomplished. No. 4 corresponds to v. 20b ("and lo,
I am with you . . .") except that the distinctive "and you shall know"
is missing.[2]

　　　With all of the above in view, Malina then describes the elements contained in 28:18b-20[3] as follows:

---

[1]Malina, 94.

[2]Ibid., 95.

[3]He calls vv. 18b-20 the "core" of vv. 16-20. V. 18a is the messenger
formula (cp. no. 1 of the outline of Cyrus' decree) "refashioned as
narrative introduction to Jesus' decree" (ibid., 94).

1. v. 18b: <u>statement of fullness of authority</u> as
   basis for command to follow and with an intima-
   tion of salvation already acquired.

2. vv. 19-20a: <u>command</u> based upon prior statement
   of authority and motivated by it.

3. v. 20b: <u>motivation</u> urging fulfillment of the
   command and functioning as a sign (proof) to
   dispel doubts.

Next, the author draws vv. 16-17 into the discussion by describing them
as the preparation and/or introduction to the authoritative decree which
follows. These preparatory verses exhibit two features: the disciples'
obedience in fulfilling the command to come to Galilee (v. 16); their
reaction when they see Jesus (v. 17). Thus, the "pattern" of the whole
pericope is as follows:

1. Fulfillment of command (v. 16),

2. Reaction[1] (v. 17),

3. Command (vv. 18-20) which begins with the messenger
   formula (v. 18a) and consists of the three elements
   just described above (vv. 18b-20).[2]

Malina's study represents the most recent and the most compre-
hensive attempt to settle the form critical problem of Mt. 28:16ff.

---

[1]To those disciples whose reaction is adoration, Jesus' command is predominantly an authoritative decree; to the doubters it is predominantly
a proof pattern ("The Literary Structure and Form of Mt. 28:16-20,"
NTS 17 (1970), 98).

[2]Ibid., 99.

Like Dodd, he studies the entire pericope, not just the actual commission, and attempts to identify its component parts. He brings to light a pericope from the HB (2 Chron. 36:23) which may, in fact, have been the type of thing[1] which influenced the composition of the Matthean passage.

The most questionable hypothesis in his study is Matthew's rather exclusive reliance on 2 Chron. 36:23 based in part on the fact of its being the final verse of the Hebrew scriptures. Malina himself admits that "the evidence for the first century A.D. is too indirect and deductive to allow for any historical certainty in the matter of the order of books."[2] Yet by the final paragraph of the article he is calling our attention, without qualification, to the fact that as the HB canon ends with Cyrus' decree for the rebuilding of Jerusalem, so Matthew's Gospel ends with Jesus' decree for the growth of the circle of disciples.[3] Two other considerations make the author's thesis uncertain: (1) K. Stendahl's work on the use of the HB in Matthew[4] has established that, although the Matthean church in its school had "access to the bulk of the Semitic Old Testament text," the LXX was the

---

[1] Our own view (see Ch. 2) is that Cyrus' decree is one of many "commissionings" which influenced Matthew. We wonder whether Malina has sought far enough for a model.

[2] Malina, 96, n. 1.

[3] Ibid., 103.

[4] The School of St. Matthew (Uppsala, 1954).

authoritatively accepted edition of the Bible in everyday church life.[1]
Since the LXX does not end with 2 Chron., most of Matthew's audience
would have missed his allusion.[2] (2) An allusion to a decree about the
rebuilding of Jerusalem seems out of place in a Gospel which interprets
the fall of that city as a judgment of God upon Jewish rejection of
Jesus.[3]

Finally, Malina's observation that 28:18-20 is also a varia-
tion of a prophetic proof pattern is likewise open to question. He
himself admits that one of the elements of the pattern is missing in
28:18-20 (no. 2). And nos. 3 and 4 are identifiable therein only with
qualifications.[4] Even more significant is the absence in the proof
pattern of any sort of commission or command. Yet the essence of the
Matthean pericope, by Malina's own admission, is a "command."[5] The
proof pattern involves an announcement of salvation from Yahweh rather
than a call to undertake a task or office for him.

---

[1] Stendahl, 205. It is curious, in this respect, that Malina himself uses
only the LXX of 2 Chron. 36 (not the MT) in comparing Cyrus' decree to
Mt. 28:16ff.

[2] On the order of books in Codex Vaticanus, see B. J. Roberts, "The Canon
and Text of the Old Testament," PCB, p. 75. There, as in Rahlf's edition of the LXX, 1-2 Chronicles follows 4 Kings and precedes 1-2 Esdras
(= Ezra-Nehemiah).

[3] See Mt. 21:33-46, 22:7. Cf. Stendahl, "Matthew," PCB, p. 791; Johnson
IB, 7, pp. 514, 516.

[4] See p. 19 above and Malina, 95.

[5] Ibid., 94, 96, 102.

III. Conclusions

After reviewing the principal contemporary studies on the literary form of Mt. 28:16-20, we still feel that an adequate solution has not been achieved. However, two of these studies are particularly instructive and have influenced our own proposed solution: those of Dodd and Trilling. The former is valuable because of its basically accurate analysis of the form critical elements in 28:16-20, the latter because it looks for a model in the HB and points to several passages in which God commissions individuals and promises his support in the undertaking. Such a model resembles Jesus' commission of the disciples (28:19-20a) which is followed by the promise of his support (20b). Still, neither Trilling nor anyone else has undertaken a systematic study of all the commissioning passages in the HB to determine whether they might provide the model for the Matthean verses under investigation. This is what we intend to do in Chapter Two to see if we can account for other elements in Mt. 28:16-20 (besides the commission and promise of support).

Chapter Two THE LITERARY FORM OF COMMISSIONS IN THE HEBREW BIBLE

I. Methodology

We are now in a position to examine the commissioning narratives in the HB to see if, in fact, they might provide a model for
Matthew's account of Jesus' commission of the disciples in 28:16-20.
Our methodology will consist of three principal steps: (1) an examination of three recent studies which deal with HB commissionings; (2) a
survey of the relevant biblical material; (3) the establishing of a
literary form (Gattung) -- based on the survey -- which can then be used
in Chapter Three to analyze the Matthean commissioning.

Before doing this, some problems of terminology have to be
ironed out. In the biblical material about to be discussed the following will always be the case. Either God or his messenger (angel, mal'āk)
or a human being is described as commissioning someone to do something
which serves to advance the progress of Israel and thereby accomplish
God's designs. Since the commission may come from God, an angel or a
man, the terms "theophany", "angelophany" or even the more general
"epiphany" cannot be used to describe generically the material with
which we are dealing. However, the vast majority of the pericopes to
be examined do, in fact, involve an epiphany. We prefer to place the
pericopes to be examined in this Chapter under the general heading of
"commissions" (or "commissionings") rather than "calls". A call connotes the initial summons of God to an individual and includes being

25

commissioned to a specific task. A commission may occur later in someone's career and may come either from God or from another man. In several of the pericopes to be studied, the commission coincides with the
initial summons (call). For this reason, we can speak of the "Call of
Abraham" (Gen. 12) or the "Call of Moses" (Ex. 3). But in other cases
a commission is given to someone already in God's service (Elijah, e.g.,
in 1 Kg. 19, or Joshua in Jos. 1). "Commission," therefore, appears to
be the broader term applicable to every pericope under investigation.

II. Relevant Hebrew Bible Studies

The form critical work of three scriptural scholars, J. Kenneth
Kuntz,[1] Norman Habel[2] and Klaus Baltzer[3] has been influential for a
determination of the categories to be used in analyzing HB commissions.
Kuntz's book is a study of HB theophanies. He defines a theophany as

> a temporal, partial and intentionally allusive self-
> disclosure initiated by the deity at a particular
> place, the reality of which evokes the convulsion of
> nature and the fear and dread of man, and whose unfold-
> ing emphasizes visual and audible aspects generally
> according to a recognized literary form.[4]

Kuntz's primary interest, then, is in the nature and form of theophanies
and is concerned with commissions only insofar as they constitute a

---

[1] The Self-Revelation of God (Philadelphia, 1967).

[2] "The Form and Significance of the Call Narratives," ZAW Band 77 Heft 3
(1965) 297-323.

[3] "Considerations Regarding the Office and Calling of the Prophet," HTR
61 (1968) 567-91.

[4] Kuntz, p. 45.

sub-category of theophanies. Thus, the theophany to Abraham in Gen.
12:1-5 involves his being commissioned (called) to start a new life in
Canaan.[1] However, when Kuntz analyzes Deutero-Isaiah, his discussion
centers entirely upon the all-pervasive theophanic language found therein with no discussion of the servant's commission (Is. 49:1-6).[2]

Another feature distinguishing the scope of this study from
Kuntz's is that he includes theophanic disclosures which evoke "the
convulsion of nature" (e.g., Pss. 18, 50 and 97). This, however, is not
a feature of the pericopes under investigation here. Nevertheless, many
of the passages studied by Kuntz will also be examined in the pages to
follow.

Using Gen. 26:23-25(J) to exemplify the theophanic *Gattung*
in what he considers its purest form, Kuntz identifies the following
formal elements of the theophany:

1.	Introductory description:	23 From there he went to Beersheba. 24 And Yahweh appeared to him the same night and said,
2.	Divine self-asseveration:	"I am the God of Abraham your father;
3.	Quelling of human fear:	Fear not,
4.	Assertion of gracious divine presence:	For I am with you,
5.	"Hieros logos"[3]	And I will bless you, and multiply your descendants for my servant Abraham's sake."

_____

[1]Kuntz, p. 116.

[2]Ibid., pp. 162-68.

[3]The *hieros logos* is "the unique word of the deity addressed to the
particularity of time and place within which the recipient stands"
(ibid., p. 68).

6. Concluding description: 25 And he built an altar
there and called upon
the name of Yahweh . . . .[1]

He goes on to emphasize that the Gattung could either expand or contract,
that it was highly flexible. In particular, the element of "an inquiry
or protest by the mortal addressed" could figure into the theophany.[2]

Habel's article is concerned with the calls of Moses, Gideon,
Isaiah, Jeremiah, Ezekiel and Deutero-Isaiah. On the basis of these
narratives, he arrives at the following call Gattung:

1. Divine confrontation: (e.g., Jdg. 6:11b-12a);[3]

2. Introductory word: (6:12b-13);

3. Commission: (6:14);

4. Objection: (6:15);

5. Reassurance: (6:16);

6. Sign: (6:17).

After demonstrating how the Gattung is employed in the other calls,
Habel concludes his study by relating the call analysis to a non-epiphanic
"commissioning" (sic) story, Abraham's command to his oldest servant that
he find a wife for Isaac (Gen. 24). Many features in the story reflect
the archaic nature of this practice: the oath ceremony (24:2-9), the
role of the servant in the patriarchal society (cf. the parallels in the
Nuzi texts), the apparent matriarchal theme (the wife must be one of

---

[1]Kuntz, p. 59.

[2]Ibid., p. 60.

[3]The verses in parentheses refer to "the archaic call of Gideon" (Habel,
298).

Abraham's kindred), and the designation "Yahweh, the God of heaven" (24:3,7).[1] According to Habel, the _Gattung_ itself is best exemplified in the servant's retelling of his commissioning to Laban and Bethuel (vv. 34-48). The breakdown is as follows:

1. _Divine confrontation:_ (missing);
2. _Introductory word:_ (vv. 34-36);
3. _Commission:_ (vv. 37f.);
4. _Objection:_ (v. 39);
5. _Reassurance:_ (vv. 40f.);
6. _Sign:_ (vv. 42-48).

The author's conclusion from all of this is that the _Gattung_ for the call of a divine representative derived from the practice exemplified in the above pericope wherein ambassadors or messengers on a special mission presented their credentials in a specific order and manner. In so doing they repeated the commission ceremony from their master including their own objections and the master's assurance that the protective angel would guide them. It was not surprising that later authors and prophets would utilize the format of this ancient practice since the prophets were seen -- or saw themselves -- as messengers commissioned by God.[2]

Although it may well be true that commissioning ceremonies such as the one in Gen. 24 provided the prototype for biblical call narratives, no attempt will be made in this study to prove this for two

---

[1] Habel, 320, n. 44.

[2] _Ibid._, 322-23.

reasons: (1) the purpose of this chapter is simply to show that a
Gattung for commissionings did exist in the HB which Matthew could have
utilized. Whether or not Gen. 24 was prototypical of this Gattung was
not Matthew's concern, and so it is not ours. (2) Gerhard von Rad,
though agreeing that swearing by the genital organ is "a very ancient
custom"[1] views Gen. 24 with its lack of specific locale, its long
speeches and its "unmistakable theological nature" as not deriving from
an ancient patriarchal tradition.[2]

Baltzer's study maintains that the primary information about
the essence and function of the prophet's office is found in the "call
and commission"[3] stories. In the calls of Isaiah, Jeremiah and Ezekiel
the following elements emerge:

1. Court audience: (e.g., Is. 6:1-4, Jer. 1:4);

2. Call: (Jer. 1:5);

3. Installation with transfer
   of authority: (Jer. 1:9);

4. Regulation of duties: (Jer. 1:10);

5. Formula of admonition: (Jer. 1:18f.) which empha-
                                  sizes the difficulty of
                                  the office, assures the
                                  prophet of God's support and
                                  requests absolute obedience;

6. Formal dismissal: (Ezek. 3:12-15).[4]

---

[1] Genesis (ET: Philadelphia, 1961), p. 249.

[2] Ibid., p. 254.

[3] Baltzer, 568.

[4] Ibid., 569-70. The examples of each element in parentheses are the
only ones supplied by Baltzer.

Baltzer then looks for a parallel to this Gattung in the literature of
the Ancient Near East. The installation of the Egyptian vizier is found
to be cast in a literary form comparable to that of the prophetic commissioning.[1] Furthermore, the actual duties of viziers have parallels
with those of Israel's prophets. Like the vizier, for example, the prophet had the responsibility of fact-finding and formulating judgment,
the execution of which was reserved to Yahweh.[2]

It will now be helpful to line up the form critical conclusions
of Kuntz, Habel and Baltzer in parallel columns so as to see better
where they agree and differ.

KUNTZ	HABEL	BALTZER
1. Introductory Description (INT)[3]		
2. Divine Self-Asseveration (CONF)[4] (see below for nos. 3 and 4)	1. Divine Confronta-tion (CONF) 2. Introductory Word	1. Court audience (CONF)

---

[1]Baltzer notes (573) that the installation of Joseph by Pharaoh in Gen.
41:39-44 follows the same pattern. The passage will be analyzed form-
critically later in this Chapter. Cf. von Rad, Genesis, p. 372: Joseph
is appointed the "grand vizier, i.e. the authorized representative of
the king himself."

[2]Baltzer, 574.

[3]A set of sigla are used in the comparative chart for two reasons:
(1) to enable the reader to compare more easily the points of similarity
between the three form critical analyses; (2) to provide the writer with
sigla which will be utilized in the analysis to follow of HB commissioning pericopes.

[4]Kuntz's divine self-asseveration will be regarded as an aspect of the
CONF because its function is that of an initial identification of the
commissioner.

5. Hieros Logos (COMM)	3. Commission (COMM)	COMM: 2. Call 3. Installation with Transfer of Authority 4. Regulation of Duties
(Inquiry or Protest by the mortal addressed)[1] (PROT)	4. Objection (PROT)	
3. Quelling of Fear (REASS) 4. Assurance of Gracious Divine Presence (REASS)	5. Reassurance (REASS) 6. Sign (REASS)[2]	5. Formula of Admonition REASS: (Among other things this assures the prophet of God's support)
6. Concluding Description (CONC)		6. Formal Dismissal (CONC)

Although the scope of each of the studies just summarized is different, there is substantial agreement on three points. (1) All speak of the moment when the deity/commissioner confronts the indiviual. (2) All emphasize the commissioning (call, hieros logos) itself. (3) All view the deity/commissioner as in some way giving reassurance or support to the one commissioned.

III. The Gattung of Commissionings

We will now examine the various commissionings found throughout the HB to see if a Gattung does exist. The three classical

---

[1] See p. 27 above.

[2] Since the function of the "sign" is to supplement the verbal reassurance with a concrete manifestation (e.g., Ex. 3:12), we will consider it a sub-element of the REASS. Habel himself says that "the concluding sign is a further confirmation of the 'I am with you' character of the assurance" (319).

divisions of the HB's Canon (law, prophets, writings) will provide the
framework. Each division will be worked through seriatim. The sigla
used above to compare elements in the form critical studies of Kuntz,
Habel and Baltzer will serve to identify the elements in the commissionings:

INT-Introduction	PROT-Protest
CONF-Confrontation	REASS-Reassurance
REAC-Reaction[1]	CONC-Conclusion
COMM-Commission	

A. Commissionings in the Law

1. Abraham's Call (Gen. 11:28-30, 12:1-4a).

INT: (28-30). The remark that Sarah was barren sets the stage for the
call itself and the promise of descendants ("a great nation"). The J
material is interrupted by the conclusion of P's genealogy (vv. 31f.).[2]

CONF: (1a). "Now the LORD said to Abram . . ."

COMM: (1b-3). The alliterative command to "go" ($le\underline{k}$-$1^e\underline{k}\bar{a}$) employs the
verb hlk which will be used again and again in commissionings. Abraham
is given the difficult mandate to abandon totally all of his natural
roots.[3]

---

[1]Although a REAC was not identified as such in any of the form critical
studies, the presence of such an element is implied in Kuntz's analysis
because of his third and fourth items ("quelling of human fear," "assertion of gracious divine presence"). Furthermore he states that ". . .
the sudden appearance of the deity is depicted again and again as an
event that evokes a keen sense of fright in the individual or group
attending such august disclosure" (p. 65).

[2]Von Rad, Genesis, 151-53. Since source criticism was unknown to Matthew,
it will not be a matter of prime concern in this study. It will be introduced only when it contributes to a significantly better understanding of
the original shape of a commissioning narrative.

[3]Ibid., p. 154.

REASS: (2b-3). Through the words of blessing Abraham is reassured that the God who makes this radical demand will remain with him. The blessing, moreover, is not limited to Abraham's descendants alone: ". . . and by you all the families of the earth shall bless themselves." Abraham will become the mediator of blessing in God's saving plan for all of the earth's families.[1] The theme of <u>universality</u> expressed here in the first commissioning narrative will reoccur frequently.

CONC: (4a). Abraham does as he is told.

      2. <u>God's Promise and Covenant with Abraham (Gen. 15:1-6)</u>.

INT: (1a). "After these things . . ."

CONF: (1b). ". . . the word of the LORD came to Abram in a vision." This kind of expression is foreign to the Torah but common in the prophetic literature (e.g., Jer. 1:4, Ez. 1:3). It is clear that the circle in which this tradition was alive imagined the theophany "as a kind of prophetic call."[2]

REASS: (1c). "Fear not . . . very great." The expression "fear not" ('al-tīrā') is common in epiphanic commissionings.

PROT: (2f.). Though the commission has not yet been given, Abraham wonders how he can possibly have a "great reward" when he remains childless.

COMM: (4-5). Abraham is called to be the father of descendants as great in number as the stars.

---

[1] Von Rad, p. 156.

[2] <u>Ibid</u>., p. 178.

CONC: (6). Abraham believes the promise and is thereby reckoned righteous.

3. Another Covenant with Abraham (Gen. 17:1-14).

INT: (1a). "When Abraham was ninety-nine years old . . . ."

CONF: (1b). ". . . the LORD appeared . . . 'I am God Almighty . . .'" This is the first occurrence of a divine self-asseveration ('^{a}nî-'el šadday).

COMM: (1c-2). The verb "walk" (hithallēk) is a form of hlk, the same root from which lēk ("go," Gen. 12:1) is derived.

REAC: (3). Abraham falls on his face.

REASS: (4a). He is reassured by hearing the words, "Behold, my covenant is with you ('ittāk)." The deity's promise to be with the commissioned individual is by far the commonest expression of reassurance in the HB, as we shall see.

COMM: (4b-14). The commission continues with the theme of universality strongly in evidence (". . . you shall be the father of a multitude of nations"). There is also added reassurance, especially in the words, ". . . and I will be their God." Finally, Abraham is given the explicit mandate of observing the covenant by the practice of circumcision.

CONC: (22-27; see #4 below).

4. Sarah's Call to be "Mother of Nations" (Gen. 17:15-27).

CONF: (15a). "And God said to Abraham . . ."

COMM: (15b-16). Through Abraham, Sarah is commissioned as "a mother of nations" (lit., in MT and LXX, "and she shall be for nations").[1] She becomes, formally, an instrument in God's designs. The reason for the change in her name from Sarai to Sarah (the former is only an archaic version of the latter)[2] is not explained in the text (contrast "Abraham," 17:5). However, it seems to add solemnity and significance to Sarah's new role and thus provide further evidence that she is, in fact, receiving a divine commission through her husband.

PROT: (17-18). Considering it impossible that his ninety-year-old wife could conceive a son, Abraham asks God to bless Ishmael. The thin line here between faith and doubt is well expressed by von Rad: "Combined with the pathetic gesture of reverence ['Abraham fell on his face'] is an almost horrible laugh, deadly earnest, not in fun, bringing belief and unbelief close together."[3]

REASS: (19-21). Abraham is reassured by hearing from God not only another promise that Sarah will bear him a son, but by learning the name which he is to call the son and by hearing that the covenant[4] will be established with him.

---

[1] E. Speiser, Genesis, Anchor Bible Vol. 1 (Garden City, N.Y.; 1964) translates: "She shall give rise to nations" (p. 123). Both this expression and the one following, "Kings of peoples shall come from her," resemble the promise to Abraham (Gen. 17:6) and the words in Jeremiah's call, "I have set you this day over nations and over kingdoms" (Jer. 1:10; cf. 1:5). In all these cases the theme of universality rings clear.

[2] Von Rad, Genesis, p. 197. Cp. Speiser, p. 125.

[3] Genesis, p. 198.

[4] The expression "my covenant" ($b^e r\hat{\imath} t\hat{\imath}$) occurs nine times in this pericope and the preceding one.

CONC: (22-27). These verses conclude the theophanic commissionings both of Abraham and Sarah. After God "went up" from Abraham, the patriarch had every male in his household circumcised.

5. The Commission of Abraham's Servant (Gen. 24:1-9).

INT: (1). Abraham is a very old man.

CONF: (2a). He addresses his most trusted servant.

COMM: (2b-4). Through the ancient practice of swearing by the genital organ, Abraham commissions the servant to find a wife for Isaac from the old country.

PROT: (5). The servant demurs that perhaps ('ûlai) the woman might not come back with him.

REASS: (6-8). Abraham assures him that "The LORD, the God of heaven . . . will send his angel before you," i.e., God will be with the servant. Furthermore, the servant's obligation ceases if the woman is unwilling to return with him to Canaan.

CONC: (9-10). The servant took the oath, then departed for Mesopotamia.

6. The Call of Isaac (Gen. 26:1-6).

INT: (1). A famine in Canaan prompts Isaac to head for Egypt.

CONF: (2a). "And the LORD appeared to him and said . . ."

COMM: (2b-5). Isaac is to dwell in Gerar. God will bless him by multiplying his descendants (cp. Abraham) and by giving him the land promised to his father. The theme of universality is again present: all the nations of the earth (kōl gôyê hā'āreṣ)[1] shall bless themselves by Isaac's descendants. The motivation for the blessings accorded to

---

[1] LXX: πάντα τὰ ἔθνη τῆς γῆς.

38

Isaac is Abraham's observance of the charges, commandments, statutes
and laws of God. This motive clause -- which is probably a later addition to the original pericope[1] -- resembles material in three other
commissionings which we will examine (Ex. 7:2, Jos. 1:1-9 and 1 Chr.
22:6-16) where Moses, Joshua and David, respectively, are told to observe all of God's commandments.

REASS: (3). ". . . and I will be with you and will bless you."

CONC: (6). "So Isaac dwelt in Gerar."

   7. A Commissioning of Isaac (Gen. 26:23-25).

INT: (23). Isaac has gone to Beersheba.

CONF: (24a). "And the LORD appeared . . . 'I am the God of Abraham
your father.'" Notice the divine self-asseveration within the confrontation.

REASS: (24b). ". . . fear not, for I am with you."

COMM: (24c). ". . . and will bless you and multiply your descendants
for my servant Abraham's sake." Although Kuntz, as noted earlier, considers this the prototypical theophany, in what sense is it a commissioning? Isaac is commissioned, in effect, to carry forward the patriarchal line. His call (Gen. 26:1-6) is here reiterated to emphasize
God's promise that his presence would accompany Isaac.[2]

---

[1]Von Rad (Genesis, p. 265) considers vv. 3b-5 as an editorial expansion.

[2]Kuntz, p. 133; cf. p. 124. There is general agreement that Gen. 26:1-6,
(except 3b-5 as already noted) and 23-25 are from the same source (J).
See Speiser, p. 203; von Rad, Genesis, p. 265; Kuntz, p. 123 (but see
his n. 41).

CONC: (25). Isaac signified his acceptance of the call by building an altar and calling upon the name of the LORD.

8. Jacob's Dream and Call at Bethel (Gen. 28:10-22).

INT: (10-12). The stage is set: Jacob dreams about a stairway reaching to heaven with angels ascending and descending on it.

CONF: (13a). Standing above the stairway, God identifies himself: "I am the LORD, the God of Abraham your father and the God of Isaac" (divine self-asseveration).

COMM: (13b-14). As with Abraham and Isaac, God promises Jacob descendants too numerous to count. The theme of universality likewise is present: "all the families of the earth" shall bless themselves by Jacob and his descendants.

REASS: (15). "Behold, I am with you . . ."

REAC: (16-17). Jacob awakes from his dream aware of the awesome presence of the deity at Bethel, and his reaction is one of fear.

CONC: (18-22). He erects a stone as a memorial column and takes a vow (cp. Isaac's actions in Gen. 26:25).

9. A Commissioning of Jacob (Gen. 35:9-15).

INT: (9). The theophany takes place on Jacob's trip home from Paddan-aram.

CONF: (10a "and God said to him . . ."; 11a "and God said to him, 'I am God Almighty . . .'"). Here the divine self-asseveration comes after the change in Jacob's name (10b).

COMM: (10b, 11b-12). Jacob is told to carry forward the patriarchal line: "be fruitful and multiply." Again there is the stress on

<u>universality</u>: an assembly of nations (ûqᵉhal gôyīm) shall come from him, as well as kings.

<u>CONC</u>: (13-15). There is a source-critical problem here. All agree that v. 13 ("God went up from him") is part of the P narrative which began at v. 9 and that v. 14 (Jacob's setting up a pillar) is E. V. 15 (Jacob's naming of Bethel) is probably P,[1] though von Rad attaches it to v. 14 as an E element.[2]

> 10. <u>Joseph's Installation as Egyptian Vizier (Gen.</u>
>   <u>41:37-45)</u>.

<u>INT</u>: (37-8). Admittedly these verses lack the circumstantial quality characterizing the previous introductions. However, they -- and the whole account of Joseph's ability to interpret dreams -- do provide the background to Pharaoh's decision to install Joseph as vizier.

<u>CONF</u>: (39a). "So Pharaoh said to Joseph . . ."

<u>COMM</u>: (39b-45b). Not surprisingly, Baltzer views this text as a good example of the installation of a grand vizier.[3] Joseph is installed in office through the word of Pharaoh. The transfer of authority is accomplished through symbolic actions: Pharaoh puts his own signet ring on Joseph's hand, arrays him in expensive garments and places a gold chain about his neck (41:42). Joseph's duties will consist of having command

---

[1]So Speiser, p. 271; Kuntz, p. 127; E. Maly, "Genesis," <u>JBC</u>, I, p. 36.

[2]<u>Genesis</u>, p. 332.

[3]P. 573. Cp. von Rad, <u>Genesis</u>, p. 372.

over all of Pharaoh's people (41:40,43).[1] Although there is no REASS

as such, the symbolic actions tend to assure Joseph of Pharaoh's com-

plete support in administering "all the land of Egypt." Finally, there

is again a change of name (cp. Abraham, Sarah and Jacob). Here it is an

act of court ceremony which draws Joseph into the Egyptian court circle.[2]

CONC: (45c). "So Joseph went out over the land of Egypt."

       11. Jacob's Journey to Egypt (46:1-5a).

INT: (1). According to 45:28, Jacob had already decided to make the

journey, and so the theophany commissioning him to do so might seem

unnecessary. Scholars are in general agreement, however, that 45:28

and at least the first half of 46:1 derive from J, whereas the remainder

of the pericope is the work of E.[3] At any rate, the text as we have it

gives the background of the commissioning: Jacob is encamped at Beer-

sheba.

CONF: (2-3a). Jacob is directly addressed by the deity who then iden-

tifies himself through divine self-asseveration.

COMM: (3b). Here there is both the immediate mandate to journey to

Egypt and a repetition of the patriarchal call theme (". . . for I will

there make of you a great nation").[4]

---

[1]As is evident from the material thus far covered and as will be seen
in many of the analyses to follow, the adjective "all" (Heb. kōl, LXX,
πᾶς) is consistently present. Sometimes, as in this instance, it
adds an emphatic note to the commissions. In other cases, it is part
of a universalistic expression (e.g., Gen. 12:3, 26:4, 28:14).

[2]Von Rad, Genesis, p. 373.

[3]Ibid., p. 396; Speiser, p. 346; Moly, JBC, I, p. 43.

[4]Cf. von Rad, Genesis, p. 397.

REASS: (4). (The words "do not be afraid . . ." in v. 3 are also part of the reassurance). Jacob is told that God will go down with him to Egypt and, in the person of his descendants, bring him back again to the promised land.

CONC: "Then Jacob set out from Beer-sheba."

12. The J and E Version of Moses' Call (Ex. 3:1-4:16).[1]

a. The J Version

INT: (3:1a-b). "Now Moses was keeping the flock . . . and he led his flock to the west side of the wilderness."

CONF: (3:2,4a,5). Initially "the angel of the LORD" is said to appear, but in verse 4a Yahweh himself is on the scene. V. 5 indicates that the place of theophany is "holy ground." The whole pattern of this theophanic narrative is reminiscent of many of the patriarchal narratives wherein God reveals himself at a specific holy place or sanctuary, especially the account of Jacob's dream at what is later to become the cult center of Bethel (Gen. 28:10-22, pericope #8 above).[2]

REAC: (3:3). Moses' reaction seems to be a mixture of curiosity[3] and amazement,[4] yet not the fear which characterizes him in the E version (3:6).

---

[1] Despite the difficulties involved in disentangling the two sources, it is felt that the Gattung can be better appreciated if this is done. M. Noth's Exodus (ET: Philadelphia, 1962) has been followed on source critical matters (see, esp., pp. 40f., 47).

[2] Noth, Exodus, pp. 38f.

[3] Kuntz, p. 144.

[4] Noth, Exodus, p. 39.

COMM: (3:7-8a ". . . to a good and broad land," 3:16-17a ". . . the affliction of Egypt"). Vv. 7-8a form a preamble to the actual word of commissioning: "Go (lēk) and gather the elders of Israel together and say to them . . ."

PROT: (4:1). Moses claims that he will not be listened to. This is the first of three attempts on his part to disqualify himself from the commission.

REASS: (4:2-9). Moses is reassured by being given the power to perform three signs (two of which Yahweh demonstrates on the spot) which will convince his peers that his mission is of divine origin.[1]

PROT: (4:10). "Oh, my Lord, I am not eloquent . . ."

REASS: (4:11-12). ". . . go (lēk, LXX: πορεύου) and I will be with your mouth (ᶜim-pîkā) and teach you what you shall speak."

PROT: (4:13). Finally, Moses simply attempts to "beg off:" ". . . send, I pray, some other person."

REASS: (4:14-16). He is told to enlist the help of Aaron and assured that, "I will be with your mouth and with his mouth."

CONC: (4:19-20a ". . . land of Egypt"). After a reiteration of the commission in v. 19 ("Go back [lēk šub] to Egypt . . ."), Moses starts back.

---

[1] J. Huesman ("Exodus," JBC, I, p. 40) comments on this passage: "God gives the answer of physical signs as assurance of the divine protection."

b. The E Version

INT: (3:1c). ". . . and came to Horeb, the mountain of God." This clause is a fragment of a more complete E introduction.[1] Notice again the mention of a specific place, Horeb.

CONF: (3:4b,6a). "God called to him out of the bush, 'Moses, Moses!' . . ." Then in v. 6a God identifies himself (divine self-asseveration) as "the God of Abraham, the God of Isaac and the God of Jacob," i.e., as the same deity who commissioned the patriarchs.

REAC: (3:6b). "And Moses hid his face, for he was afraid to look at God." Cp. Jacob's fear in Gen. 28:17.

COMM: (3:9-10). V. 9 is the preamble (the oppression of the sons of Israel), v. 10 the commission per se (seek their release from Pharaoh).

PROT: (3:11). "Who am I that I should go to Pharaoh . . ." In E Moses' protest stems from his existential condition as a fugitive (cf. Ex. 2:11ff.).[2]

REASS: (3:12). "But I will be with you . . ." The promise of a sign provides further reassurance.[3]

PROT: (3:13). Moses wants to know God's name.

REASS: (3:14-15). In seeking to know it, Moses is looking for added reassurance. He will only be able to convince the people of Israel of the genuineness of his theophanic encounter if he is able to tell them the name of the deity.

---

[1] Noth, Exodus, p. 38.

[2] D. Stalker, "Exodus," PCB, p. 212.

[3] On the difficult question of what this sign really consists of, cf. Noth, Exodus, p. 42.

CONC: (4:18). Moses asks Jethro's permission to go back to Egypt.

13. Another Commission of Moses (Ex. 6:2-13,7:1-6).[1]

CONF: (6:2-3). "And God said to Moses, 'I am the LORD (^{a}nî yhwh)'"
(divine self-asseveration). He then explains that he had not been known
to the patriarchs as yhwh but as 'el šadday.[2]

COMM: (6:4-8, 10-11). Vv. 4-5 are a preamble to the commission itself
(cp. Ex. 3:9). Moses is first told to deliver a message of salvation
to the sons of Israel (vv. 6-8), but their enslaved condition causes
them to ignore him (v. 9). Secondly Moses is to "tell" (dabbēr) Pharaoh
to let the people go.

PROT: (6:12). Since the Israelites would not listen to him and since
he is a man of "uncircumcised lips," i.e., incompetent as a speaker,
Moses does not see how Pharaoh will listen.

REASS: (6:13, 7:1). After reiterating the commission (6:13) -- and
thus leaving no doubt about the matter -- Yahweh gives Aaron to Moses
as his prophet (spokesman, cp. Ex. 4:14-16). With Aaron as his prophet,
Moses is now "God (^{e}lōhîm)" with respect to Pharaoh, i.e., possesses
God's authority.

---

[1]The section from 6:14-27 is a genealogical insertion into the narrative.
Vv. 28-30 then briefly recapitulate 6:2-13 with the addition of the
explicit circumstantial detail that the commission took place in Egypt.
Cp., esp., vv. 12 and 30. Noth, Exodus, p. 58.

[2]Just as God has, in effect, changed his own name from God Almighty to
Yahweh, he changed Abram's name to Abraham (Gen. 17:5), Sarai's to
Sarah (17:15) and Jacob's to Israel (35:10). The sections containing
these changes (which seem to symbolize a new relationship between God
and man) are almost universally attributed to P.

COMM: (7:2-5). With the exception of 7:2a, these verses are difficult to identify simply as a continuation of the commissioning. In the sense that they promise deliverance from Egyptian bondage (vv. 4f.), they provide reassurance to Moses. V. 7:2a contains several key commissioning words, some of which have already been commented upon: "You shall speak ('attāh t^e dabbēr) all that I command you (ēt kol 'a^{y}šer '^{a}sawwekā).[1] The verb "to command" (ṣwh in the piel) will occur in a number of pericopes hereafter.

CONC: Moses and Aaron did as they were commanded.

14. Balaam's Commission (Num. 22:22-35).

INT: (22-30). In the long circumstantial introduction, Balaam's ass perceives the angelophany but the diviner himself sees nothing.

CONF: (31a). Through divine assistance, Balaam finally saw (wayyar')[2] the angel.

REAC: (31b). ". . . and he bowed his head and fell on his face." Cp. the similar reactions of Abraham (Gen. 17:3) and Moses (Ex. 3:6).

CONF: (32-33). Balaam is informed of his perversity and of how close he came to being slain.

REAC: (34). He confesses his guilt. Cp. Is. 6:5.

COMM: (35a). He is to "go with" (lēk ^{c}im)[3] Balak's men but to speak only the word (ēt-haddābār)[4] which the angel bids him to speak.

---

[1] LXX: πάντα, ὅσα σοι ἐντέλλομαι. ἐντέλλομαι is the normal LXX equivalent of ṣwh.

[2] Cp. Is. 6:1.

[3] LXX: συμπορεύθητι.

[4] Note the importance of dābār in the calls of the classical prophets, e.g., Jer. 1:4,9; Ezek. 1:3, 3:4.

CONC: (35b). "So Balaam went on with the princes of Balak."

15. The Commissioning of Joshua (Dt. 31:14-15, 23).[1]

INT: (14). The circumstances behind Joshua's commissioning are presented: since Moses soon will die, a successor is needed.

CONF: (15). Yahweh appears in the tent of meeting in a pillar of cloud.

COMM: (23). Although Moses is the intermediary, God himself performs the commissioning.[2] The verb for "commission" in vv. 15 and 23 is ṣwh in the piel (LXX: ἐντέλλομαι).[3]

REASS: (23). The expression, "be strong and of good courage (ḥªzaq we'emāṣ)," occurs both here and in Joshua's other commissioning which follows below. The reassurance -- and the pericope -- closes with Yahweh's emphatic, "I will be with you (we'ānōḵî 'eheyeh ʿimmāḵ)." The expression rounds off the pericope and thus serves as a conclusion. Another reason for the lack of the usual type of conclusion is that Joshua cannot fulfill his commission to lead the Israelites into Canaan until Moses' death.[4]

---

[1]The divine mandate that Moses write a song which will serve as a witness against the people when they turn to other gods (vv. 16-22) interrupts the commissioning narrative. Cf. J. Blenkinsopp, "Deuteronomy," JBC, I, p. 120; von Rad, Deuteronomy (ET: Philadelphia, 1966), 188-89.

[2]LXX of v. 23, however, reads, "and Moses commissioned Joshua . . ." Although MT literally reads, "and he commissioned Joshua . . .," the context makes it very clear that God, not Moses, is being referred to (particularly the expression, "I will be with you").

[3]Cp. Ex. 7:2.

[4]See N. Lohfink, "Die deuteronomistische Darstellung des Übergangs der Führung Israels von Moses auf Josue," (Scholastik 37, 1962, 32-44), for a form critical analysis of this pericope, the one to follow (Jos. 1:1-11) and Dt. 31:7-8. It resembles the analysis presented here.

B. Commissionings in the Prophets

1. Joshua's Other Commissioning (Jos. 1:1-11).

INT: (1a). The death of Moses provides the setting for this commissioning.

CONF: (1b). "the LORD said to Joshua . . ."

COMM: (2-4, 7-8). Joshua is commissioned (1) to begin the conquest by taking the people across the Jordan; (2) to do all that is commanded in the book of the law. The use of two key "commissioning" words should be noted. (1) The verb ṣwh (LXX: ἐντέλλομαι), "command," is employed in vv. 7 and 9. (2) In the discussion of Gen. 41:37-45[1] it was pointed out that the adjective kōl (LXX: πᾶς), "all," is frequently employed in commissionings. In the pericope before us, it is found six times (MT and LXX).

REASS: (5-6, 9). As Yahweh was with Moses, so will he be with Joshua. The expression, "be strong and of good courage," is used in vv. 6 and 9. In v. 9 it is the positive side of the expression which follows it: "be not frightened, neither be dismayed."

CONC: (10-11). Joshua begins preparations for the crossing of the Jordan.

2. The Commissioning of Barak (Jdg. 4:4-10).

INT: (4-5).[2] "Deborah . . . was judging Israel at that time."

CONF: (6a). She summons Barak into her presence.

---

[1] P. 40, n. 1.

[2] V. 5 is probably an editorial insertion. J. N. Schofield, "Judges," PCB, p. 307.

COMM: (6b-7). "The Lord . . . commands (ṣiwwāh)[1] you, 'Go (lēk) gather your men . . .'"

PROT: (8). Barak responds that he will not go into battle without Deborah.

REASS: (9a-b). She replies, "I will surely go with you . . ."

CONC: (9b-10). Deborah goes forth with Barak to Kedesh. He then gathers his army in accordance with his commission.

3. The Commissioning of Gideon (Jdg. 6:11-24).

INT: (11). Under the oak at Ophrah, Gideon is secretly beating out wheat in the wine press so as to hide it from the Midianites.

CONF: (12). Yahweh's messenger "appeared" (wayyērā') and speaks an initial word of assurance: "The LORD is with you."

PROT: (13). Gideon wonders how Yahweh can be with the Israelites when they are being dominated by the Midianites.

COMM: (14). As in the J version of Moses' call (Ex. 3:4a), the messenger steps into the background and Yahweh himself tells Gideon to "go" (lēk, LXX: πορεύου) and rescue Israel from Midian.

PROT: (15). Now Gideon argues that the commission is impossible for someone as lowly as he.

REASS: (16). "But I will be with you, and you shall smite the Midianites as one man."

---

[1]LXX: ἐνετείλατο.

<u>PROT</u>: (17-18). Gideon requests a "sign" to reassure him that he is speaking with God. For if he is, then the conquest of Midian is no longer in doubt.[1]

<u>REASS</u>: (21). The angel carries out the sign by igniting Gideon's present.

<u>REAC</u>: (22). Gideon is struck with awe at having seen God's messenger face to face.

<u>REASS</u>: (23). Yahweh himself reassures him: ". . . <u>do not fear</u> ('al tîrā'), you shall not die."

<u>CONC</u>: Gideon builds an altar to the Lord.[2]

4. The Call of Samuel (1 Sam. 3:1-4:1a).

<u>INT</u>: (3:1-3). Samuel is ministering to God under Eli at a time when Yahweh's word is rare.

<u>CONF</u>: (3:4-11a). As with Moses (Ex. 3:4), God calls (wayyiqrā') with the double direct address, "Samuel, Samuel" (1 Sam. 3:4,10). The narrator adds suspense (and humor) to the account by having Samuel not recognize divine summons until Eli finally perceives the fact. At the moment of recognition Samuel responds, "Speak, for thy servant (ᶜabdeka)[3] hears."

<u>COMM</u>: (11b-14). Since Samuel is simply told that punishment is about to come upon the house of Eli, the pericope might appear as primarily an

---

[1]Habel, 301. Cp. the sign phenomenon in Ex. 4:1-9 (the J version of Moses' commission).

[2]Cp. Gen. 26:25, 28:18-19.

[3]Cp. the use of ᶜebed in Jos. 1:1,2 (referring to Moses) and in Is. 49: 3,5,6 (referring to the "servant").

announcement of that fact. Although it does have this function, its deeper purpose can be seen from a look at the whole account. (1) It is a theophany in which God encounters Samuel in a manner similar to his meetings with the patriarchs, Moses, Gideon and the classical prophets. (2) Samuel is pictured as one capable from boyhood of receiving the "word" and "vision" of the Lord (1 Sam. 3:1, 4:1a).[1] (3) Vv. 3:19-4:1a describe Samuel as "a prophet of the Lord" who received divine revelations and whose word (d^{e}bar) was heeded in Israel. "The Lord was _with him_" (3:19). As von Rad observes, ". . . whatever office the historic Samuel actually held, what the narrator wished to relate was the way in which a young man was raised up as a prophet (v. 20)."[2] We conclude, then, that the text describes Samuel's call to the office of prophet.

PROT: (3:15). It would be almost as accurate to describe the verse as a REAC. Samuel recoils in fear from the task of telling Eli, his master, that he and his house will be punished.[3]

REASS: (3:16-18). Although the verses might appear more threatening than reassuring, Samuel is being assured by Eli that the latter really wants to know what God has said.

---

[1] H. Hertzberg, _I and II Samuel_, (ET: Philadelphia, 1964), p. 41: ". . . the chapter depicts as it were the call of Samuel."

[2] _Old Testament Theology_, V. II (ET: New York, 1965), p. 55. J. Turro, "1-2 Samuel" _JBC_, I, p. 166 agrees with von Rad and Hertzberg.

[3] Like Isaiah of Jerusalem ("Here am I! send me," Is. 6:8), Samuel's initial readiness changes to reluctance ("How long, O Lord?", Is. 6:11).

CONC: (3:19-4:1a). The verses reemphasize Samuel's prophetic vocation by stating that he began to practice as a prophet. They also round off the pericope.

5. Elijah's Flight and Reassurance (1 Kg. 19:1-19a).

INT: (1-9a). Elijah's flight from Jezebel is described, which finally takes him to a cave on Mt. Horeb.

CONF: (11b-12).[1] The "still small voice" contains God's presence rather than the wind, earthquake or fire.

REAC: (13a). In the presence of deity Elijah wraps his face in his mantle, much as Moses had hidden his face (Ex. 3:6).

CONF: (13b). The silence is broken by Yahweh's question: "What are you doing here, Elijah?"

PROT: (14a). Elijah complains about Israel's infidelity and Jezebel's attempt to murder him.

COMM: (15-17). Elijah is to "go, return" (lēk šûb)[2] and anoint Hazael as king of Syria, Jehu as king of Israel and Elisha as his own successor.

REASS: (18). God announces that seven thousand faithful Israelites will be spared. This gives comfort to the prophet who sees himself as standing alone.

CONC: (19a). Elijah departs and finds Elisha.

------

[1]Because vv. 9b-11a break the flow of the narrative and are needlessly repetitious, most scholars consider them a secondary insertion. Kuntz, p. 147, n. 21; cf. P. Ellis, "1-2 Kings," JBC, I, p. 195; J. Mauchline "1-2 Kings," PCB, p. 346.

[2]LXX: πορεύου ἀνάστρεφε. Cp. Ex. 4:19.

6. The Inaugural Theophany to Isaiah of Jerusalem (Is. 6).

INT: (1a). "In the year that King Uzziah died . . ."

CONF: (1b-4). Isaiah receives a vision of the holy God surrounded by the seraphim.

REAC: (5). The prophet reacts with a realization of his corresponding unholiness ("For I am lost; for I am a man of unclean lips . . .").

REASS: (6-7). The symbolic purification of the prophet with a burning coal reassures him that his sin is forgiven.

COMM: (8-10). He is commissioned to "go" (lēk LXX: πορεύθητι) and carry out the paradoxical mission of making the heart of the people fat and their ears heavy, and of shutting their eyes.

PROT: (11a). "How long, O Lord?"

COMM: (11b-13b). The commission is repeated in variant terms which leave no doubt in Isaiah's mind as to its duration. These poetic final verses also form a sort of CONC by solemnly rounding off the pericope.

Habel includes the disputed final line of v. 13 ("The holy seed is its stump.") as authentic since the reassurance it provides is consistent wich such an element in many other call narratives.[1] It is very possible, however, that the statement is a gloss intended to soften the grim commission which Isaiah received from the God of Israel. Its position at the very end of the Isaian call narrative adds credence to

---

[1]Habel, 312. Other scholars who uphold its authenticity include: von Rad, OT Theology, II, p. 64; J. Lindblom, Prophecy in Ancient Israel (ET: New York, 1965), pp. 186f.; I. Engnell, The Call of Isaiah (Uppsala, 1949), pp. 47f.

this view. Therefore it seems preferable not to bolster the evidence
for the presence of the commissioning form in Is. 6 by appeal to this
chronically disputed final sentence.[1]

      7. <u>The Call of Jeremiah (Jer. 1:1-10)</u>.[2]

<u>INT</u>: (1-3). In the strictest sense this is not an introduction but an
editor's preface which introduces the ent*i*re prophecy and not just the
call thereto. However, it does tell us when "the word of the Lord"
first came to Jeremiah (the thirteenth year of King Josiah's reign),
and it probably replaced an original and more specific historical note.[3]

<u>CONF</u>: (4). "Now the <u>word</u> of the Lord came to me saying, . . ."

<u>COMM</u>: (5). Yahweh announces that Jeremiah has been appointed "a
prophet to the nations" (nābî' laggôyîm) from the beginning of his

---

[1]Scholars who consider it a gloss include: J. Bright, "Isaiah-I," <u>PCB</u>,
p. 495; R. B. Y. Scott, "The Book of Isaiah: Chs. 1-39," <u>IB</u>, 5, pp.
212-13; S. Blank, "Traces of Prophetic Agony in Isaiah," <u>Hebrew Union
College Annual</u> 27 (1956), 86.

[2]Although only vv. 1-10 are included in this analysis (the call <u>per se</u>),
it is obvious that the remainder of Ch. 1 (vv. 11-19) with its two visions
and final word of reassurance is closely related to the call. For this
reason certain germane features in vv. 11-19 will be mentioned. J. P.
Hyatt, "Jeremiah," <u>IB</u>, 5, p. 805, suggests that the two visions probably
came to the prophet "at the time of his call or in the days which immediately followed." Exegetes who agree that the call account ends with
v. 10 are: Hyatt, p. 791; Habel, 306; J. Paterson, "Jeremiah," <u>PCB</u>,
p. 541. Those who disagree are: Baltzer, 569 and G. Coutourier,
"Jeremiah," <u>JBC</u>, I, pp. 304-5. The general criterion followed in this
study with respect to visions is that they must be a part of the initial
confrontation which is followed by the commission if they are to be included in the commissioning <u>per se</u>. Thus, although Jeremiah's visions
are not included, Ezekiel's are (see below).

[3]Habel, 307. Cf. Paterson, <u>PCB</u>, p. 541.

existence. The theme of universality appears both here and in v. 10

where the prophet is given authority "over nations and over kingdoms."[1]

PROT: (6). Jeremiah, somewhat like Moses (Ex. 4:10, 6:12), tries to

excuse himself because of lack of ability to speak.

COMM: (7). This verse employs three terms frequently encountered in

commissionings: ". . . for to all (kol) to whom I send[2] you shall go

(telēk), and whatever (w^e'e̱t kol '^{a}šer)[3] I command ('^{a}ṣaww^{e}ka̱) you shall

speak."

REASS: (8-9). In v. 8 the language is again typical: "be not afraid

('al tîra̱') of them for I am with you . . ." In v. 9 the symbolic

touching of the prophet's mouth by Yahweh provides additional assurance

that his words are now Jeremiah's to speak.[4]

This is a suitable place to comment on the special use of

another word frequently found in commissionings, "behold" (hinnēh, LXX:

ίδού), since it occurs twice in the material being discussed. This

---

[1]Cp. Gen. 17:6, 16; 35:11: kings shall come forth from Abraham, Sarah
and Jacob. As von Rad notes (Genesis, pp. 194-5), the Ishmaelites,
Edomites and sons of Keturah are not primarily meant but all those to
whom God's plan of salvation would extend through Israel. The same is
true with Jeremiah's commission.

[2]"Send": 'ešlah^{a}ka̱. Cp. the use of šlh in Moses' commissioning, Ex.
3:10, 12.

[3]LXX: "and whatever" (καὶ κατὰ πάντα, ὅσα) I command you (ἐὰν
ἐντείλωμαί σοι) . . ." Cp. Ex. 7:2 and Jer. 1:17 where the wording
is nearly identical.

[4]Cp. Is. 6:7, Ezek. 2:8-3:3. Habel (309) remarks on Jer. 1:9: "This
action provided additional confirmation that Jeremiah was a mediator
who could receive the divine word itself."

particle has a high frequency in the HB, and actually occurs four times
in Jer. 1. However, only in vv. 9 and 18 is it used by the commissioner
and in conjunction with the pronoun "I." When used in this way it draws
attention to what the commissioner is doing vis-a-vis the one commissioned: "Behold, I have put (hinnēh nātattî) my words in your mouth."[1]

COMM: (10). The poetic final verse rounds off (and thus concludes)
the call and further specifies the prophet's duties.[2]

After the supplemental visions in vv. 11-16, material from the
COMM and REASS are repeated in vv. 17-19 including what Baltzer identifies as "elements of proverbial wisdom" in a prophetic call: ". . .
behold, I make you this day a fortified city, an iron pillar and bronze
walls, against the whole land . . ." (v. 18; cp. Ezek. 2:6, 3:8-9). The
proverbial wisdom was part of the "formula of admonition" in the installation of an Egyptian vizier.[3]

---

[1] The following are the other uses of "Behold, I . . ." in pericopes we
have examined or will examine (an asterisk indicates that the personal
pronoun ('anî or 'anokî) is expressed and not just contained in the verb):
Gen. 17:4,* 20; 28:15;* Num. 22:32;* 1 Sam. 3:11;* Ezek. 3:8. In addition the LXX of Gen. 41:41 and Jer. 1:10 employs ἰδού to translate
Heb. re'ēh ("see," "behold"). J. Muilenburg, "Form Criticism and Beyond,"
JBL, 88 (1969), notes that hinnēh sometimes appears "in striking contexts"
(14).

[2] In the preceding footnote, the use of re'ēh in both Gen 41:41 and Jer.
1:10 was mentioned. In both places, moreover, the commissioner sets
the individual (Joseph, Jeremiah) over (ᶜal) a certain jurisdiction.

[3] Baltzer, 569, 572.

8. <u>The Call of Ezekiel (Ezek. 1:1-3:15)</u>.[1]

<u>INT</u>: (1:1-3). The prophet's call occurs at a specific time and place: July 28, 593 B.C.E., by the River Chebar in Babylon.[2]

<u>CONF</u>: (1:4-28a). The theophany is reminiscent of Isaiah's (Is. 6:1-4): the Lord is seated upon a throne attended by superhuman creatures so that his "glory" (k^e bod, Is. 6:3, Ezek. 1:28) is experienced. However, Ezekiel adds a wealth of detail to his description which emphasizes the motifs of brightness, fire, thunder, etc.

<u>REAC</u>: (1:28b). "And when I saw it, I fell upon my face . . ."[3]

<u>REASS</u>: (2:1-2). The Spirit enters Ezekiel enabling him to stand up again, thus providing him with reassurance and enabling him to encounter the word of Yahweh.

<u>COMM</u>: (2:3-5). Like Moses and Jeremiah, Ezekiel is "sent" (šlḥ, 2:3,4; 3:5,6) by God on his mission.

<u>REASS</u>: (2:6-3:3). The familiar "be not afraid" ('al-tîrā') is employed three times in 2:6 to reassure the prophet in his mission to the "rebellious house" of Israel. Although no PROT as such is to be found in the commissioning narrative, one is implied from the way in which Yahweh insists that Ezekiel is neither to fear (2:6) nor be rebellious himself

---

[1]We will view 1:1-3:15 as a literary unit. So Muilenburg, "Ezekiel," <u>PCB</u>, pp. 571f.; W. Zimmerli, <u>Ezechiel</u> (Neukirchen, The Netherlands; 1969), pp. 13-37. Ch. 1 remains "a torso" without 2:1-3:15 (Zimmerli, p. 35). In the HB, descriptions of visions are never an end in themselves.

[2]Muilenburg, "Ezekiel," p. 571. Cp. Is. 6:1.

[3]Cp. Gen. 17:3, Ex. 3:6, 1 Kg. 19:13.

(2:8).[1] The symbolic act or "sign" wherein the prophet eats the scroll with the words of lamentation and mourning upon it and experiences its sweet taste _assures_ him that Yahweh's words are sweet to those who willingly accept them.[2]

COMM: (3:4-11). The commission is reiterated: "go, get you (lek̲-bō')[3] to the house of Israel, and speak with my words to them." There is an emphatic stress in Ezekiel on hearing and speaking the word(s) of Yahweh (1:3, 2:7, 2:8-3:3, 3:4, 3:11).[4] Yet "the house of Israel will not listen" for they are "of a hard forehead and a stubborn heart."[5]

In 3:8-9 a note of reassurance is sounded in Yahweh's statement that he has hardened Ezekiel's face to withstand Israel's hardness. It is another example of the "proverbial wisdom" feature first seen in Jeremiah (see also Ezek. 2:6).

CONC: (3:12-15). The theophany closes amid the sound of a great earthquake. The Spirit transports the prophet to the location of the exiles where his career will begin.

---

[1]Habel, 313.

[2]Muilenberg, "Ezekiel," p. 572. Cp. Jer. 1:9 where, however, the stress is on the authority which possession of God's word conveys rather than on the sweetness resulting from assimilation of them.

[3]The technical term lēk is also used by the commissioning deity in 3:1 and 3:11.

[4]Cp. Jer. 1:2, 4, 7, 9, 11, 12, 13, 17; 1 Sam. 3:10.

[5]Cp. Is. 6:9-11.

9. The Call of the "Servant" (Is. 49:1-6).[1]

INT: (1a). It is not surprising in a poetic composition such as
Deutero-Isaiah that a circumstantial introduction would be lacking.
Instead, the servant summons "peoples (LXX: ἔθνη, but MT l^e'ummîm)
from afar" to listen to the account of his commissioning.

COMM: (1b-2). Like Jeremiah (Jer. 1:5) he is called from the womb.

CONF: (3a). "And he said to me . . ."

COMM: (3b). "You are my servant . . ."

PROT: (4). The servant complains that he has "labored in vain." An
element of REASS is present, also, but on the servant's own lips:
". . . my right is with the LORD and my recompense with my God.

COMM AND REASS: (5-6). The final section of the COMM is inextricably
woven together with words of reassurance: the servant has already been
"honored" with a mission to Israel (v. 5); now it is extended to all
the nations of the earth (v. 6). As with the calls of Isaiah and
Jeremiah, there is no CONC as such, but the poetry of this second Servant song appropriately concludes the pericope.

-----

[1]This is the one instance where a pericope is not taken seriatim. It
seemed advisable in view of the general scholarly agreement that Is.
40-55 was composed after Ezek. and Jer. It does not appear necessary
to make a decision in this study on the much-disputed question of the
servant's identity. Whether he is the anonymous author of Is. 40-55
(which seems unlikely; see von Rad, Theology, II, pp. 259-62), a
future individual, the corporate Israel (or a faithful remnant thereof)
or, in some sense, both the corporate Israel and a future individual,
the description of a commissioning would not be out of place. C. Westermann, Isaiah 40-66 (ET: Philadelphia, 1969) observes on this question:
"On principle, their exegesis [that of the four Servant songs] must not
be controlled by the question, 'Who is this servant of God?' Instead
we must do them justice by recognizing that precisely this is what they
neither tell nor intend to tell us" (p. 93).

The theme of universality begins with the opening verse summoning coastlands and peoples to listen. It reaches its climax in the famous expression, "I will give you[1] as a light to the nations (gôyīm, LXX: ἐθνῶν) that my salvation may reach to the end of the earth."

C. Commissionings in the Writings

1. David's Commissioning of Solomon to Build the Temple (1 Chron. 22:1-16).

INT: (1-5). "Before his death" David provides men and material for the building of the temple.

CONF: (6-7a). ". . . David said to Solomon . . ."

COMM: (7b-10). David describes to his son how "the word of the LORD" had come to him, and explains that not he but Solomon would build the temple.

COMM and REASS: (11-16). The two elements are interwoven in these verses. There are several similarities between this pericope, especially vv. 11-16, and Joshua's commissioning (Jos. 1:1-11). (1) As Moses' mission was completed by Joshua, David's task of constructing the temple is turned over -- after elaborate preparation -- to Solomon.[2] (2) Solomon, like Joshua, is to observe the law of Moses, its statutes and ordinances (Jos. 1:7-8, 1 Chr. 22:12-13). (3) The technical verb ṣwh ("command," "charge") occurs in both (Jos. 1:7, 9; 1 Chr. 22:6, 12, 13).

---

[1]LXX, only, has "Behold (ἰδοὺ) I will give you . . ."

[2]R. North, "The Chronicler: 1-2 Chronicles, Ezra, Nehemiah," JBC, I, p. 412; cf. von Rad, Theology, I, p. 351.

(4) The expressions of reassurance are identical in Hebrew or nearly so: "The LORD be with you" (1 Chr. 22:11,16; cp. Jos. 1:9); "Be strong and of good courage" (1 Chr. 22:13; Jos. 1:7,9); "Fear not; be not dismayed" (1 Chr. 22:13, Jos. 1:9).

CONC: (16b). The words, "arise and be doing! The Lord be with you", conclude David's speech and round off the account of the commissioning.

    2. <u>Cyrus' Commissioning of the Jews in Babylon to Rebuild the Temple (Ezr. 1:1-5, 2 Chron. 36:22f.).</u>[1]

INT: (1). Cyrus' proclamation takes place during the first year of his rule in Babylon (538).[2]

CONF: (2a). "Thus says Cyrus king of Persia: . . ." Unlike every other pericope studied, there is no direct confrontation between commissioner and commissioned. Instead, a proclamation from Cyrus is both publicly heralded and officially posted (v. 1).[3] In this way, the word of Cyrus confronts the Jewish exiles.

COMM: (2b-4). V. 2b-c forms the background to the commission proper by stating that the Lord has given Cyrus <u>all</u> (kōl) the kingdoms of the

---

[1]R. North ("The Chronicler: 1-2 Chronicles, Ezra, Nehemiah," <u>JBC</u>, I, p. 428) thinks that at one time 1 Chronicles 36:22f. continued directly into what is now Ezr. 1:4. When the Ezra scroll was separated and inserted into the Jewish canon before there was felt to be any need for Chronicles, these two verses were borrowed to stand at the start of Ezra. Cp. O. Eissfeldt, <u>The Old Testament: An Introduction</u> (ET: Oxford, 1965), pp. 530f.

[2]North, <u>Ibid.</u>; J. Myers, <u>Ezra-Nehemiah</u>, Anchor Bible V. 14 (New York, 1965), pp. 5f.

[3]Myers, p. 6.

62

earth and charged him to build the Lord a house at Jerusalem.[1] Both the
use of "all" here in v. 2 and again in v. 3 ("Whoever is among you of
all his people . . .") are hyperbolic.[2] They thus differ somewhat from
the traditional uses of "all" in previous pericopes. Similarly, the
typical commissioning verb, "go" (hlk), is absent. In its place is a
jussive form of ^{c}lh: "let him go up."

REASS: (3). ". . . may his God be with him . . ." This expression
resembles the "I am with you" spoken by God, but is obviously not identical since Cyrus is speaking.

CONC: (5). The family heads, priests and Levites respond to the commissioning and begin preparations for their task.

IV. Conclusions

A. The Nature of the Gattung Elements

We are now in a position to analyse the nature of each of the
formal elements found in commissionings.

1. _Introduction._ Almost invariably there is a brief introductory remark providing circumstantial details (time, place, etc.)
which set the stage for what is to follow. Only two[3] of the twenty-seven
pericopes studied were without an INT.

2. _Confrontation._ The deity/commissioner then comes on the
scene to address the individual to be commissioned. In several pericopes

---

[1]Cp. the words about building the Lord a house to similar expressions
in the previous pericope (1 Chron. 22:2, 6, 7, 10, 11).

[2]Cf. Myers, pp. 7 f.

[3]Gen. 17:15, Ex. 6:2 (see, however, Ex. 6:28).

in Genesis and Exodus,[1] the deity describes himself by means of the
formula, "I am . . ." (= Kuntz's "divine self-asseveration"). No pericope lacks a CONF.[2]

3. <u>Reaction</u>. In eight instances[3] the individual reacts to
the presence of the deity or his angel by way of an action expressive
of fear or unworthiness.

4. <u>Commission</u>. The individual is told to undertake a
specific task which often involves his assuming a new role in life
(e.g., that of prophet). This, obviously, is the central element in
the literary form which is found in all twenty-seven pericopes.

5. <u>Protest</u>. In thirteen[4] of the pericopes the individual
responds to the commission by claiming that he is unable or unworthy to
accomplish it, or by questioning the word of the deity/commissioner in
some way.

The two elements appearing with the least frequency are the
PROT (13) and the REAC (8). However, one or the other of them occurs in

---

[1] Gen. 17:1, 26:24, 28:13, 35:11, 46:3; Ex. 3:6, 6:2.

[2] Ezr. 1:1-5 is a possible exception in that Cyrus does not directly con-
front the exiled Jewish community and commission them to rebuild the
temple. However, the proclamation of his heralds accomplishes the same
thing.

[3] Gen. 17:3, 28:16f.; Ex. 3:3,6; Num. 22:31; 1 Kg. 19:13; Is. 6:5; Ezek.
1:28. The relationship of the REAC to the PROT will be discussed below.

[4] Gen. 15:2, 17:17, 24:5; Ex. 3:11; 4:1, 10, 13; 6:11, 30; Jdg. 4:8, 6:13,
15; 1 Sam. 3:15; 1 Kg. 19:14; Is. 6:11, 49:4; Jer. 1:6. We also noted
an implied PROT in Ezek. 2:6-8.

seventeen different pericopes out of twenty-seven. Only five commissioning accounts have both.[1] It appears that there is a general tendency to
have the individual respond either to the presence of the commissioner
(REAC) or to his commission (PROT).

      6. Reassurance. Only three pericopes[2] lack this feature.
The commissioner's word of reassurance usually is spoken after the COMM
(and after the PROT, if there is one). Occasionally it is spoken at the
beginning of the narrative in response to a REAC of fear or unworthiness
on the part of the person confronted. In a few cases,[3] a sign supple-
ments the verbal reassurance.

      7. Conclusion. The commission usually concludes in a more
or less formal way, most often with a statement that the one commissioned
starts to carry out his work. Of the four pericopes in which a specific
CONC could not be isolated, three were in material from the classical
prophets (Is. 6:11b-13b, 49:5f.; Jer. 1:10).[4] In each of these cases,
we maintained that the poetic nature of the final verse(s) served to
round off and thus conclude the account.

      So as to summarize our findings graphically, we now present a
schematization of the use of the Gattung in the twenty-seven pericopes
studied. Parentheses around an 'x' indicate that the element in question is not present in the usual sense or is present only by implication.

---

[1] Ex. 3:1-4:16 (J), Ex. 3:1-4:16 (E), Jdg. 6:11-24, 1 Kg. 19:1-19a, Is. 6.

[2] Gen. 35:9-15; Gen. 41:37-45 (though, as noted, vv. 42f. describe symbolic actions on Pharaoh's part which would function to reassure Joseph);
Num. 22:22-35.

[3] Ex. 3:12, 4:2-9; Jdg. 6:17f., 21; Is. 6:6f.; Ezek. 2:8-3:3.

[4] The other pericope without a CONC is Dt. 31:14-15, 23. It, too, has a
sort of CONC (see p. 46 above).

	INT	CONF	REAC	COMM	PROT	REASS	CONC
LAW:							
Gen. 11:28-30, 12:1-4a	x	x		x		x	x
Gen. 15:1-6	x	x		x	x	x	x
Gen. 17:1-14	x	x	x	x		x	x
Gen. 17:15-27		x		x	x	x	x
Gen. 24:1-9	x	x		x	x	x	x
Gen. 26:1-6	x	x		x		x	x
Gen. 26:23-25	x	x		x		x	x
Gen. 28:10-22	x	x	x	x		x	x
Gen. 35:9-15	x	x		x			x
Gen. 41:37-45	x	x		x		(x)	x
Gen. 46:1-5a	x	x		x		x	x
Ex. 3:1-4:16 (J)	x	x	x	x	x	x	x
Ex. 3:1-4:16 (E)	x	x	x	x	x	x	x
Ex. 6:2-13, 7:1-6	(x)	x		x	x	x	x
Num. 22:22-35	x	x	x	x			x
Dt. 31:14f., 31	x	x		x		x	(x)
PROPHETS:							
Josh. 1:1-11	x	x		x		x	x
Jdg. 4:4-10	x	x		x	x	x	x
Jdg. 6:11-24	x	x	x	x	x	x	x
1 Sam. 3:1-4:1a	x	x		x	x	x	x
1 Kg. 19:1-19a	x	x	x	x	x	x	x
Is. 6	x	x	x	x	x	x	(x)
Jer. 1:1-10	x	x		x	x	x	(x)
Ezek. 1:1-3:15	x	x		x	(x)	x	x
Is. 49:1-6	x	x		x	x	x	(x)
WRITINGS:							
1 Chron. 22:1-16	x	x		x		x	x
Ezr. 1:1-5	x	x		x		x	x

B. Repetition of Elements

We have noticed that the COMM may be reiterated later in a pericope, and that the PROT and the REASS sometimes appear more than once in a pericope. In the J version of Moses' call, e.g., there are three protests each of which is countered by Yahweh's word of reassurance. The fact that repetition occurs and that most of the pericopes studied do not contain all seven elements[1] makes it clear that the Gattung was not monolithic. It was used in the service of the biblical authors. However, the Gattung persists in documents whose span of composition stretches from the Jahwist to the Chronicler.

C. Reoccurrence of Themes

Not only the Gattung itself but specific themes reoccur in the material studied. The theme of universality appears in five of the Genesis pericopes[2] and twice in the classical prophets.[3] In six of the commissionings[4] stress is put on observance of God's commandments. In six cases Moses either plays a part or is expressly mentioned.[5] In nearly all the pericopes the theme of God's continual protective presence is in evidence.

---

[1] The only ones that do are the J and E versions of Moses' call (Ex. 3:1-4:16), Gideon's commission (Jdg. 6:11-24) and Elijah's commission (1 Kg. 19:1-19a).

[2] Gen. 12:1-4a, 17:1-14, 17:15-22, 26:1-6, 28:10-22.

[3] Jer. 1:1-10, Is. 49:1-6.

[4] Gen. 26:1-6, Ex. 6:2-7:7, Jos. 1:1-11, Jdg. 4:4-10, Jer. 1:1-10, 1 Chron. 22:1-16.

[5] Ex. 3:1-4:16 (J and E), 6:2-7:7; Dt. 31:14-15, 23; Jos. 1:1-11; 1 Chron. 22:1-16.

D. Reoccurrence of Technical Words and Phrases

Finally, certain expressions are characteristic of commissionings: "I am (will be) with you,"[1] "fear not," "be strong and of good
courage," "behold (I)," "go,"[2] "I command," "I send," "the word (of
Yahweh)," "all,"[3] etc. As we have seen, the consistent use of the same
or similar Hebrew expressions in pericopes from diverse parts of the HB
further attests the existence of a commissioning Gattung.

E. The Significance of the Commissioning Accounts

It goes almost without saying that the pericopes analyzed are
very significant ones. They describe how Israel's patriarchs and prophets were summoned (via the commissioning formula) to participate in
events which shaped the people's destiny.

---

[1]"I am (will be) with you" or an equivalent expression occurs in 15 of
27 pericopes, sometimes more than once: Gen. 17:4, 19, 21; 24:7; 26:3;
28:15; 46:4; Ex. 3:12; 4:15; Dt. 31:23; Jos. 1:5, 9; Jdg. 4:9; 6:12, 16;
Jer. 1:8 (cf. 1:19); 1 Chron. 22:11, 16; Ezr. 1:3.

[2]In thirteen pericopes the idiomatic expression, "go", (usually hlk,
LXX πορεύομαι) forms part of the commission: Gen. 12:1; 24:4;
Ex. 3:16; 6:11; Jos. 1:2; Jdg. 4:6; 6:14; 1 Kg. 19:15; Is. 6:9; Jer. 1:7;
Ezek. 3:11; Ezr. 1:3.

[3]"All" (kōl, LXX πᾶς) appears in 10 pericopes, sometimes more than
once: Gen. 12:3; 26:4; 28:14; 41:40f.; Ex. 7:2; Jos. 1:2, 5, 7; Jer.
1:7 (twice); Ezek. 2:10; 1 Chron. 22:9; Ezr. 1:2f.

Chapter Three MATTHEW 28:16-20:

A FORM CRITICAL AND EXEGETICAL ANALYSIS

I. The Gattung of 28:16-20

We have demonstrated in Chapter Two the existence of a HB commissioning Gattung and of characteristic words and phrases which accompanied it. We shall now attempt to show that Matthew was significantly influenced by the Gattung and its vocabulary when he composed the missionary charge in 28:16-20.[1] Thus the breakdown of these verses may be schematized as follows:

INT (16) Now the eleven disciples went to Galilee to the mountain to which Jesus had directed them.

CONF (17a) And when they saw him . . .

REAC (17b) . . . they worshipped him; but some doubted.

CONF (18) And Jesus came and said to them, "All authority in heaven and on earth has been given to me.

---

[1]Matthew is profoundly influenced by the HB throughout his Gospel. He directly cites it 44 times, 20 of which are not derived from his Markan source nor found in Luke. Of these 20, 10 are found in no other NT book. J. McKenzie, "The Gospel according to Matthew," JBC, II, p. 64; cf. Johnson, IB, 7, p. 233. Matthew was also influenced by rabbinic thought, e.g., in his use of the terms "teach" and "name." A study of this, however, is beyond our scope. Cf. Stendahl, School, pp. 30-35 and his Bibliography; and see below, p. 92, n. 2.

COMM (19-20a) "Go, therefore, and make disciples of

all nations, baptizing them in the name

of the Father and of the Son and of the

Holy Spirit, teaching them to observe

all that I have commanded you;

REASS (20b) ". . . and lo, I am with you always,

to the close of the age."

The INT consists of the typical circumstantial detail: the disciples have gone to Galilee for the rendezvous with Jesus.

The CONF is in two stages. First, the eleven catch sight of Jesus from a distance.[1] Secondly, after the worship and doubt of the disciples (to which we will return momentarily), Jesus approaches them and speaks. His opening words identify him as the unique possessor of the universal authority (πᾶσα ἐξουσία) of God.[2] Jesus is saying, in effect: "I am the One to whom God has given all authority in heaven and on earth." So these words perform a function similar to the divine self-asseveration ("I am the God of . . .") which occurred in seven of the HB pericopes as a sub-element of the CONF.[3]

---

[1] See W. Grundmann, Das Evangelium nach Matthäus (Berlin, 1968), p. 576, who describes the disciples as being "at a certain distance" from Jesus.

[2] Blair, Jesus, p. 140. P. Gaechter in Das Matthäus Evangelium (Innsbruck, 1963), p. 964, remarks on 28:18: "The passive form [ἐδόθη μοι] serves here, as often, as a paraphrase of an action of God."

[3] Gen. 17:1, 26:24, 28:13, 35:11, 46:3, Ex. 3:6, 6:2. See Chapter Two, p. 62.

The disciples' worship and doubt comprise the REAC in the commissioning. Προσκυνέω (worship) connotes prostration before and adoration of a deity.[1] The element of prostration related it to the action of falling (to the ground) on one's face seen in the REAC of three HB commissioning narratives.[2] Worship is the natural reaction of men who recognize that Jesus is the risen Messiah. Doubt (at least on the part of some) is also not surprising in view of the epiphanic character of the situation.[3] The Jesus whom they see has died and now is risen. They wonder whether it can really be he (cp. Lk. 24:37, 41).[4]

The COMM is to make disciples of all men everywhere through baptism and instruction in Jesus' commandments. The REASS is the "I am with you" formula so common in HB commissionings.

There is no CONC in the usual sense of the commissioned individuals' going forth to do what they have been told. Instead, Matthew brings the pericope and his entire Gospel to a conclusion with the risen Jesus' words that he will be with the disciples always "to the close of the age." The phrase forms a suitable end to the Gospel for several reasons. (1) By closing the commissioning account at this point,

---

[1] Heinrich Greeven, "Προσκυνέω," TDNT, VI, p. 759. He notes that the literal meaning of the word is simply to "kiss reverently."

[2] Gen. 17:3, Num. 22:31 (προσεκύνησεν in LXX), Ezek. 1:28; cf. Jdg. 13:20 and Dan. 10:9.

[3] Lohmeyer, Matthäus, p. 415, n. 3.

[4] See P. Bonnard, L'Évangile selon St. Matthieu (Paris, 1963), p. 418, who maintains that all NT Christophanies leave room for doubt because they are not events of an objectively material sort.

Matthew leaves his reader with a sense of the enduring presence of the
risen One to his disciples and of them to him. (2) The First Gospel is
addressed to a Christian community which looks back upon the missionary
work accomplished by the first disciples. Matthew, therefore, is not
interested in relating the self-evident fact that the disciples went
and did as commanded. He is interested in telling the Christians of his
day that the presence of the risen Jesus will endure. (3) The words of
commissioning have a poetic quality which would be broken by a final
statement that the disciples went and did as commanded. In this respect
the pericope resembles three HB commissionings (Is. 6, Is. 49:1-6 and
Jer. 1:1-10) which are poetic and which, as noted, come to an appropriate
close without a CONC in the technical sense. (4) The phrase also forms
an appropriate ending because Matthew consistently looks ahead to the
eschatological day when Jesus, who had never deserted his people,[1]
would be present in glory to judge the world.[2] Jesus does not ascend
to heaven (contrast Lk. 24:51, Mk. 16:19) nor do the disciples set out
to accomplish their mission. The openness of the scene thus corresponds
to the author's method of composition (e.g., in the missionary discourse
in Mt. 10 where the scene also remains open).[3]

---

[1]See 1:23, 10:32, 18:20, 28:20.

[2]Johnson, IB, 7, p. 625 who cites 25:31-46 in support.

[3]G. Barth, "Matthew's Understanding of the Law," TIM, p. 133, n. 2.
See below, p. 174, n. 2, regarding Matthew's use of a CONC in 28:8,11
(the angelophany and Christophany to the women at the tomb).

II. An Exegesis of 28:16-20

A. The Mountain in Galilee (28:16)

Although both the angel (28:7) and Jesus himself (28:10) had told the women simply to have the eleven disciples meet Jesus in Galilee, we now learn (28:16) that they were to rendezvous with him on a mountain. As the typical site of revelations in the First Gospel,[1] it has "mythological rather than geographical significance."[2] Since Acts 1:12 indicates that Jesus spoke his final words to the disciples from the Mount of Olivet, Matthew may have derived the mountain theme from the tradition.[3] However, the mythological use to which Matthew puts the theme and the lack of mention of a specific mountain (as in Acts 1:12) make it appear much more likely that the mountain is a Matthean addition to the commissioning tradition known to him.[4]

---

[1]G. Bornkamm, "Der Auferstandene und der Irdische, Mt. 28:16-20," in E. Dinkler (ed.) Zeit und Geschichte (Tübingen, 1964), p. 171, who compares it with Mt. 5:1, 15:29, 17:1.

[2]Stendahl, PCB, p. 698; cf. McKenzie, JBC, II, p. 113.

[3]G. Barth, TIM, p. 132, considers this possible.

[4]Marxsen, The Resurrection of Jesus of Nazareth (ET: Philadelphia, 1970), p. 47, argues from the lack of mention of the mountain in 28:1-10 that Matthew found it in the tradition. Yet the reverse seems to be true. Matthew takes the reference to a meeting in Galilee (28:7, 10) from Mark 16:7 where no mountain is mentioned. In 28:16 Matthew himself adds the reference to the mythological mountain. "It would in any case be hazardous to conclude that Matthew had before him a narrative of an appearance on a mountain, for the narrative elements are minimal" (Fuller, p. 81).

B. The Confrontation with the Risen One (28:17a)

No description of the risen Jesus is given. We learn only that "when they saw him" they both worshipped and doubted. Bornkamm argues from this that the entire scene should not be described as an epiphany narrative.[1] In support he cites Dibelius who considers that epiphanies contain the element of the miraculous (an element missing from 28:16-20) as an "end in itself" (Selbstzweck).[2] Bornkamm also notes the absence of any description of how Jesus appears or disappears, of the fear or joy of the disciples or of their recognition of him.[3]

Since Bornkamm's observations are accurate for the most part, it is necessary to distinguish a full-blown epiphany narrative from a narrative which only states the fact of the epiphany. In Mt. 28:17f. the bare fact of the Christophany is stated, followed by the missionary charge. In the same way, some of the HB epiphanic commissionings are characterized by a lack of descriptive detail. The CONF in them simply states the fact that God has appeared: "The LORD appeared to Abram and said . . ." (Gen. 17:1); "and the LORD appeared to him [Isaac] and said . . ." (Gen. 26:2).[4] Admittedly, there are other epiphanic commissionings in which the descriptive details are present.[5]

---

[1]"Der Auferstandene . . .," p. 172.

[2]Dibelius, Formgeschichte, p. 91.

[3]"Der Auferstandene . . .," p. 172. By contrast, Bornkamm notes the presence of one or another of these elements in Lk. 24:25ff., 31ff., Jn. 20:16, 20.

[4]Other examples are: Gen. 12:1, 26:24, 35:9f.; Ex. 6:2f.

[5]Most notably, Gen. 28:12f., Ex. 3:2ff., Dt. 31:15, Is. 6:1ff., Ezek. 1.

We do disagree with Bornkamm that 28:16-20 says nothing about the disciples' recognition of Jesus. Their recognition is described in the statement in 28:17: "And when they saw him they worshipped him; but some doubted."

C. The Worship and Doubt of the Disciples (28:17b)

When the NT uses προσκυνέω, the object is always something -- truly or supposedly -- divine. Matthew has prepared for its use here by stating that the Magi worshipped the child Jesus (2:11) and by altering or expanding his Marcan source in five places so as to describe the gesture of those who approach Jesus as προσκύνησις (8:2, 9:18, 14:33, 15:25, 20:20).[1] The most significant preparation for its use in 28:17, however, is the way the women at the tomb are described as worshipping Jesus (28:9).[2] As in 28:17ff., the gesture of worship is contained within a commissioning story: the women are told by the risen Jesus to have the disciples meet him in Galilee (28:10).[3]

The disciples' doubt has been a controversial exegetical question. Only a few scholars maintain that a group distinct from the eleven disciples is meant.[4] Some feel that all eleven see Jesus, all

---

[1]Greeven, TDNT, VI, p. 763.

[2]The identical form, προσεκύνησαν, is used in 28:9 and 17. See F. Neirynck, "Les Femmes au Tombeau," NTS 15 (1968-9), 178f.

[3]A comparative analysis of the two commissionings is given on pp. 173f. below.

[4]A. H. McNeile, The Gospel According to St. Matthew (London, 1915), p. 484; W. C. Allen, A Critical and Exegetical Commentary on the Gospel according to St. Matthew (New York, 1924), p. 305.

worship and all doubt.[1] Others argue that only some among the eleven

doubt.[2] This position has the best grammatical support,[3] and is, there-

fore, probably the safest opinion to follow. However, it should not be

inferred from this that Matthew thinks the doubters were without faith.

Διστάζω, as used in both classical and koine Greek, indicates that

a person is divided in his conviction and cannot make up his mind whether

to believe or not. Faith exists, but it is imperfect.[4] Διστάζω

is used only one other time in the entire NT: Mt. 14:31, the report of

Jesus' walking on the water and Peter's faltering attempt to go out of

the boat to him. As Jesus rescues Peter he asks, "0 man of little

faith, why did you doubt (ἐδίστασας)?" As they get into the boat,

the wind subsides and the disciples worship (προσεκύνησαν) him

(14:33). Thus, διστάζω is associated here also with προσκυνέω

in a pericope which, like 28:16-20, is epiphanic in character.[5] Further-

more, Matthew has added both these verbs in this extensive redaction of

Mark's stilling of the storm (Mk. 6:45-52).

---

[1]Grundmann, p. 576; Bonnard, p. 418, who writes, "The worship was not
without some hesitation and a certain inner anguish."

[2]Stendahl, PCB, p. 798; F. Filson, The Gospel according to St. Matthew
(New York, 1960), p. 305; Malina, NTS 17, 98; Neirynck, NTS 15, 180,
n. 1.

[3]Bl.-Debr., #250: "In these two places [Mt. 26:67, 28:17] no differ-
entiation is mentioned at the beginning of the sentence, but with the
appearance of οἱ δὲ it becomes evident that what was said first did not
apply to all."

[4]I. P. Ellis, "But Some Doubted," NTS 14 (1967-68), 576. Johnson comments that, ". . . we are not to suppose that all disciples had perfect
faith." (IB, 7, p. 621).

[5]Ellis, NTS 14, 578f.

We will see in Chapter Four that the juxtaposition of disbelief and joy or awe was an element in the common tradition behind the
commissioning accounts in the four Gospels. In Matthew, however, this
phenomenon is expressed in language characteristic of his Gospel:
διστάζω (doubt) and προσκυνέω (worship). The description of
the disciples' worship and doubt may have been intended to impress upon
Matthew's readers the difficulty of faith in the event of Easter and yet
the need for it.[1] What alone overcomes the doubt is the words of
Jesus (vv. 18-20).[2]

D. The Approach of Jesus (28:18a)

Before Jesus begins to speak, he approaches the disciples.
Only twice in the First Gospel is the term προσέρχομαι ("approach,"
"come") applied to Jesus: here and in another text unique to Matthew
(17:6f.) which is part of his redaction of the Markan transfiguration
account. Both times Jesus approaches the disciples who are prostrate
before him and reassures them.[3]   A comparison between the two texts
points out the parallels and adds weight to several points already made
about the vocabulary of 28:16-20.

17:6-7	28:16-20
When the disciples heard this,	Now the eleven disciples . . . and when they saw him.

---

[1]Cf. G. Barth, TIM, p. 133; Bornkamm, "Der Auferstandene . . .," p. 172;
Michel, "Der Abschluss . . .," 16ff.

[2]Bornkamm, ibid.

[3]Neirynck, NTS 15, 180.

they fell on their faces, and were filled with awe.	they worshipped him; but some doubted.
But Jesus came καὶ προσῆλθεν ὁ ᾿Ιησοῦς	And Jesus came καὶ προσελθὼν ὁ ᾿Ιησοῦς
and touched them, saying,	and said to them,
"Rise and have no fear."	"All authority . . . I am with you always . . ."

The parallel between "they worshipped" and "they fell on their faces" strengthens the equivalence already made between these expressions.[1]

Since "doubted" (28:17) and "feared greatly" (17:6)[2] are also parallel, the ambivalent character of διστάζω (belief mixed with unbelief) can again be seen.

ἐλάλησεν αὐτοῖς λέγων is paralleled in passages where Matthew has redacted his Markan source to produce this particular formulation (lit., "Jesus spoke to them saying . . .").[3]

E. The Declaration of Authority (28:18b)

1. ᾿Εξουσία

The expression, "All authority in heaven and on earth has been given to me," was previously identified as part of the CONF and as similar to the "divine self-asseveration." The term "authority" (ἐξουσία), applied frequently by Mark to describe the quality of Jesus' teaching and work is -- with one exception -- reproduced by

---

[1]P. 69.

[2]RSV: "were filled with awe."

[3]Mt. 13:3, 14:27, 23:1; in agreement with Strecker, Weg, p. 209.

Matthew.[1] He adds ἐξουσία to his Markan source at one point:

". . . they glorified God who gives such authority to men" (9:8, cp.

Mk. 2:12). In addition, Matthew reproduces the cry of jubilation (11:27,

Lk. 10:22; Q) in which Jesus states that all things have been delivered

to him by his Father. This plus the repeated affirmations of Jesus'

messiahship are caught up in the expression in 28:18.

A comparison of the cry of jubilation (11:27) with 28:18 and

Jn. 3:35 reveals several verbal parallels.

Mt. 11:27a (Q, cp. Lk. 10:22)	Mt. 28:18b	Jn. 3:35
All things (πάντα) have been delivered (παρεδόθη) to me (μοι) by my Father (πατρός).	All authority (πᾶσα ἐξουσία) in heaven and on earth has been given to me (ἐδόθη μοι).	The Father (πατὴρ) loves the Son and has given (δέδωκεν) all things (πάντα) into his hand.

More importantly, the three passages run parallel in their assertion

that Jesus is the recipient of divine prerogatives. Jn. 3:35 and the

Q saying reflected in Mt. 11:27a were influenced by LXX Dan. 7:14.[2] In

turn, 11:27a affected the composition of 28:18b.[3] The further question,

---

[1]Mk. 1:22=Mt. 7:29; Mk. 2:10=Mt. 9:6; Mk. 6:7=Mt. 10:1; Mk. 11:28, 29, 33=Mt. 21:23, 24, 27. The one exception is Mk. 1:27. Matthew omits the whole pericope (Mk. 1:23-8, the cure of a demoniac at Capernaum), or perhaps telescopes it with the story of the Gadarene demoniac (Mt. 8:28-34). Blair, p. 46.

[2]Fuller, p. 83; Blair, p. 47 (who discusses only Mt. 11:27).

[3]Blair, p. 67. He notes -- in addition to the verbal parallels -- the delegation of authority from Father to Son in both places and the echo of the phrase "heaven and earth" (= Mt. 11:25, where the Q saying begins) in 28:18 ("all authority in heaven and on earth") as reasons. Cf. H. Tödt, The Son of Man in the Synoptic Tradition (ET: Philadelphia, 1965), pp. 258f.

to which we turn now, is whether LXX Dan. 7:14 more directly influenced
the composition of 28:18b.

In Chapter One[1] we evaluated the theory of Michel and Jeremias
that 28:18-20 is a triple-action coronation text modeled on LXX Dan.
7:13-14. Although, for reasons presented there, the idea has not been
generally accepted, many scholars[2] think that at least v. 14 of Dan. 7
has influenced the composition of 28:18b. To evaluate the question
better, the verbal parallels are set forth below.

Dan. 7:14a   Mt. 28:18b-19a

καὶ ἐδόθη αὐτῷ   ἐδόθη μοι

ἐξουσία   πᾶσα ἐξουσία

καὶ πάντα τὰ ἔθνη   ἐν οὐρανῷ καὶ

τῆς γῆς κατὰ γένη   ἐπὶ [τῆς] γῆς

καὶ πᾶσα δόξα   πορευθέντες οὖν μαθητεύσατε

αὐτῷ λατρεύουσα·   πάντα τὰ ἔθνη...

The exact nature of the relationship between the two texts
has been examined by Tödt and Trilling whose conclusions necessitate
caution in any comparison of the Danielic and Matthean pericopes.

---

[1]Pp. 7-9.

[2]These include: Fuller, p. 83; Filson, p. 305; McNeile, p. 435;
Lohmeyer, Matthäus, pp. 416f.; Bonnard, p. 418; G. Barth, TIM, p. 133.

Tödt, although granting that there is an allusion to Dan. 7:14 in Mt.
28:18, feels that this allusion is specifically to the concept of enthronement -- not the concept of the Son of Man. If Matthew had meant
to present Jesus as the "Son of Man," he could not have omitted the
designation itself.[1] This view is substantiated, he feels, by comparing
Mt. 28:18 to 26:64 (par. Mk. 14:62). In 28:18 the risen Jesus speaks
about his installation to Lordship as an accomplished fact ("all authority . . . has been given to me"). In 26:64, on the other hand, the
Son of Man's coming in power is predicted by Jesus as a future event,
the parousia: "Hereafter you will see the Son of Man seated at the
right hand of Power, and coming on the clouds of heaven." Nevertheless,
Tödt has perhaps overlooked one fact of eschatology. When Jesus speaks
of his possession of all authority in 28:18, the parousia and the con-
sequent exaltation of the Son of Man are still future realities. "The
close of the age" (28:20) has not yet arrived. Consequently, Jesus
cannot be expected to say something like, "I am the Son of Man," nor
can he come on the clouds of heaven (cf. 24:30, 26:64). Yet, for the
present, his possession of universal authority (28:18) enables him to
exercise the functions of Son of Man as completely as possible.[2]

Trilling notes that the Matthean text lacks the features of
a court presentation found in Dan. 7:13f. (the bringing of the Son of

---

[1] Tödt, p. 288. Cp. the similar view of Hahn, p. 66, n. 3.

[2] Cf. Fuller, p. 83, n. 22.

Man before "the Ancient of Days" and the worship of him by all nations.)[1]
Also -- as we noted in Chapter One[2] -- the Matthean pericope deals primarily with Jesus' authoritative commission, not with his personal reception of authority (contrast Daniel) which is an accomplished fact.

The foregoing discussion would seem to indicate that Matthew did draw freely upon language from LXX Dan. 7:14 to frame Jesus' statement of authority. Attempts to draw any further conclusions appear unwarranted.

2. ". . . in heaven and on earth"

The expression, "heaven and earth," as used in the First Gospel, describes the whole universe. Yet the emphasis is sometimes on the distinction between heaven and earth (the sphere of God and that of man)[3] and sometimes on the unity of the two spheres.[4] In both 11:25 and 28:20 the unity of the two spheres is expressed. In the former verse, the Father is described as "Lord of heaven and earth;" in the latter, Jesus is described as having been given the universal authority of the Father.

---

[1]Trilling, p. 23.

[2]P. 9.

[3]5:34f., 6:10, 6:19f., 16:19, 18:18. Cp. 18:19, 23:9. There are no parallels in Mark or Luke to these uses.

[4]5:18 (=Lk. 16:17), 11:25 (=Lk. 10:21), 24:34 (=Mk. 13:31), 28:18. Trilling, pp. 24f. In the latter sense (unity of heaven and earth) the phrase is used in one of the HB commissioning accounts studied (Gen. 24:3, "The LORD, the God of heaven and of the earth." Ezr. 1:2 (the commissioning by Cyrus) reads: "the LORD, the God of heaven, has given me all the kingdoms of the earth . . ." See also Dan. 4:14 (LXX,B) and Ezr. 5:11.

In summary, v. 18a contains Matthean redactional language (προσελθὼν . . . ἐλάλησεν αὐτοῖς λέγων); v. 18b reflects the influence (both directly and via Mt. 11:27a) of LXX Dan. 7:14.

F. The Missionary Command (28:19a)

1. Πορευθέντες

In Chapter Two we noted the recurrence of the idiomatic expression, "go" (MT: hlk, LXX: usually πορεύομαι), in commissionings.

Here, as in the HB, the emphasis does not fall on the participial πορευθέντες ("go"), but the imperative, μαθητεύσατε ("make disciples"). Nevertheless, the sense of mission is emphasized by πορευθέντες in a way which parallels the participial use of this verb in the commissioning of the Twelve in 10:7: πορευόμενοι δὲ κηρύσσετε ("and preach as you go").[1] An even closer verbal parallel to 28:19a (πορευθέντες οὖν μαθητεύσατε) occurs in Mt. 9:13a where Matthew has added to Mark's account of a dispute between Jesus and the Pharisees Jesus' words "Go and learn (πορευθέντες δὲ μάθετε) what this means, 'I desire mercy, and not sacrifice.'"[2]

---

[1] Note the use of the imperative form, πορεύεσθε, in 10:6. Both uses are redactional additions to Mark. Malina (NTS 17, 90) concludes from the participial use of πορεύομαι in 28:19 that to speak of. the command as a "missionary command" is inaccurate. ". . . the core of the command is to make disciples not to go." Although this is true, it would seem that if the eleven were to make disciples of all nations, a very extensive mission must have been envisioned by Matthew.

[2] Note the following additional uses of πορεύομαι both of which are unique to Matthew and involve a commissioning of some sort: 2:20 (angel to Joseph), 28:7 (angel to women). The fact of the association of πορεύομαι four times (2:20, 10:7, 28:7 and 20) with commissioning pericopes in redactional contexts leads to the conclusion that the commissioning language of the HB influenced Matthew at several points in his Gospel.

The conjunction, οὖν ("therefore"), is typically Matthean.[1] Here it is very significant because it connects the grounds for Jesus' prerogative of commissioning ("all authority") to its corollary: his ability to commission the disciples for their universal task of disciple-making.

2. Μαθητεύσατε

Although μαθητής (disciple) is very common in Matthew and in the NT generally, the related verb, μαθητεύω, is very rare. It occurs only four times, three of which are in Matthew (13:52, 27:57, 28:19). The active sense of "making disciples" is found only in 28:19 and Acts 14:21.[2]

3. Πάντα τὰ ἔθνη

The identical expression, πάντα τὰ ἔθνη, is used three other times in the First Gospel, and in each case the meaning is the same: all nations (Jews and gentiles) without distinction.[3] Jesus tells his disciples that they will be "hated by all nations for my name's sake" (24:9). This is a redaction of the Markan source: "and you will be hated by all (ὑπὸ πάντων) for my name's sake" (Mk. 13:13).[4] However, in 13:10 Mark has: "And the gospel must first be preached to all nations: (εἰς πάντα τὰ ἔθνη). Matthew alters this somewhat: "And this gospel of the kingdom will be preached

---

[1]See Mt. 5:48; 6:8f., 31, 34; 7:12, etc.

[2]Bl.-Debr.,#148, 3. The verb is used deponently at 13:52 and 27:57, and as an intransitive active in the variant reading of 27:57.

[3]Cf. K. L. Schmidt, "Ἔθνος in the NT," in TDNT, II, p. 369; Trilling, pp. 26-28; W. G. Kümmel, Introduction to the New Testament, pp. 81f.

[4]Hahn, p. 120.

throughout the whole world as a testimony to all nations" (πᾶσιν
τοῖς ἔθνεσιν, 24:12). The expression, "throughout the whole
[inhabited] world" (ἐν ὅλῃ τῇ οἰκουμένῃ) further emphasizes
universalism. The phrase is taken over by Matthew from colloquial
Hellenistic Greek and denotes the inhabited earth. It has a political
and legal connotation which fits in well with the legal sense contained
in "as a testimony (εἰς μαρτύριον) to all nations" (24:14).[1]
Finally, in the Matthean parable of the last judgment (which has no
parallels), the Son of Man is pictured as sitting on his throne with
"all the nations" (πάντα τὰ ἔθνη) (25:32) gathered before him.

Besides the expressions employing "all nations," Matthew also
prepares for the universal missionary theme in 28:19 by his use of the
term κόσμος (world). In the interpretation of the parable of the
weeds (parable and interpretation found only in Mt.), Jesus explains
that "the field is the world." The term indicates an unqualified universalism extending to Jews and gentiles alike.[2] A similar use of
κόσμος occurs in 26:13 (=Mk. 14:9) where Jesus states that his
anointing by the woman at Bethany will be remembered "wherever this
gospel is preached in the whole world." In 5:14 the disciples are
called "the light of the world." They have a mission to give light to
the world by their example (cf. 5:16).[3]

---

[1]Michel, "Οἰκουμένη," TDNT, V, pp. 159f.

[2]Trilling, p. 126.

[3]Stendahl, PCB, p. 776; Grundmann, Matthäus, p. 139.

In one of the "formula" quotations, 12:18-21, Matthew's universalism also appears. Here he quotes Is. 42:1-4 and identifies Jesus with the Servant who "proclaims justice to the Gentiles" and in whose name the "Gentiles hope." Finally, the story of the Magi (2:1ff.) points proleptically to the enlargement of the idea of the people of God to include all peoples.[1]

Thus Matthew has prepared in various ways for the command to make disciples of all nations. Once again the final verses of the Gospel recapitulate an important theological idea contained in the body of the work.

Two principal factors seem to have influenced the universalism at the close of the First Gospel. (a) A universalistic emphasis is frequently to be found in the HB.[2] This is true with respect to the commissioning material analyzed in Chapter Two. In seven of the pericopes[3] the theme of universalism is mentioned, and in five of these

---

[1]Bornkamm, "Der Auferstandene . . .," p. 189. Cf. Johnson, IB, 7, p. 256.

[2]E.g., Is. 2:1-4, 18:7, 42:1-4, 45:22, 60:1-3; Jer. 3:17, 16:19; Zeph. 3:8-11; Zech. 2:10f., 8:20-23; Dan. 7:14 (see earlier discussion, pp. 33,65); Ps. 86:9. See Hahn, pp. 19ff.; Jeremias, pp. 56ff.

[3]Gen. 12:1-4a, 17:1-14, 17:15-22, 26:1-6, 28:10-22; Jer. 1:1-10; Is. 49:1-6. LXX Gen. 26:4 uses the identical πάντα τα ἔθνη of Mt. 28:19 (as does a non-commissioning passage, Gen. 22:18). In the Genesis material, the individuals in question (Abraham, Isaac, et al.) are commissioned to follow the God of Israel and accept the patriarchal role. By so doing, they will bring blessings on "all the nations." In Is. 49:6 and Jer. 1:5, there is a more direct missionary charge to be "a light (prophet) to the nations." On the influence of these two prophetic calls on the call of Paul (Gal. 1; Acts 9, 22, 26), see Munck, Paul and the Salvation of Mankind (ET: Richmond, Va., 1959), pp. 27ff. Munck rightly stresses the way that the mission to the nations in the calls of Jeremiah and Deutero-Isaiah has affected the manner in which Paul understood his

seven the LXX employs ἔθνη (nations).[1] (b) We have concluded in

Chapter Four[2] that the mission to "all nations" was part of an original

commissioning tradition which underlies the Easter commission narrated

by Matthew, Luke, John and the author of the longer ending of Mark

(16:9-20).

G. The Baptismal Command (28:19b)

Probably the most disputed feature of 28:16-20 is the authen-

ticity of the triadic[3] baptismal formula, "baptizing them in the name

of the Father and of the Son and of the Holy Spirit." One patristic

writer, Eusebius of Caesarea, cites 28:19 frequently without the baptis-

mal command. Because of the complexity of the Eusebian data and of the

contemporary discussion of the issue, we have treated it separately in

Appendix Two. Arguing principally from an analysis of Eusebius' in-

exact method of quoting the NT and from the complete lack of manuscript

evidence for a variant reading, we have there concluded that the tria-

dic baptismal command is most probably authentic.

---

missionary call. See, in particular, Gal. 1:15 (cp. Is. 49:1, Jer. 1:5);
Acts 26:17 (cp. Jer. 1:7f.); Acts 26:18 (cp. Is. 42:6, LXX 42:7). Cf.
also Ezr. 1:2 where Cyrus says that the Lord has given him "all the kingdoms of the earth," and charged him to build the Jerusalem temple.

[1]Gen. 12:3 and 28:14 have πᾶσαι αἱ φυλαὶ τῆς γῆς ("all the families
of the earth"). LXX is consistent in translating ἔθνη for Heb.
gōyīm (nations) and φυλαί for Heb. mišpᵉḥôt (families).

[2]Pp. 112-15.

[3]The term "triadic" seems preferable because trinitarian theology deve-
loped out of the early Church's belief in the triadic activity of God
as Father, as Son and as Spirit. See Strecker, Weg, p. 209, n. 6.

The disciples are enjoined by Jesus to carry out their mission of disciple-making both by baptizing into the threefold name and by teaching new followers to observe all of Jesus' commandments.[1] Matthew thus exhibits in 28:19b-20a an interest in the church or community. Trilling characterizes this aspect of the commission as the Gemeindeordnung (regulation of the community) which is preceded by the Missionsauftrag (the missionary charge itself): "Go, make disciples of all nations" (28:19a).[2] Two other Matthean pericopes explicitly discuss the regulation of the community, in both of which the word ἐκκλησία ("church," "community") itself is used.[3] In 16:17-19 Matthew adds to Peter's confession (derived from Mk. 8:27-9) the blessing upon him (16:17) followed by the designation of him as the "rock" upon which Jesus' ἐκκλησία would be built (v. 18). Then come the symbolic words about giving Peter the keys of the kingdom so that he can bind and loose, i.e. exercise authority as the church's leader.[4]

The second pericope, 18:15-17 also unique to Matthew,[5] describes the exact procedure by which one Christian was to correct another who had sinned against him. If private correction (v. 15) and

---

[1] G. Barth, TIM, p. 135. As Trilling puts it: "The μαθητής [disciple] is one who has been baptized and who observes the commands of Christ" (p. 40).

[2] Trilling, p. 40.

[3] 16:18, 18:17 (twice). These are the only uses of ἐκκλησία in the four Gospels. Luke, however, employs the word frequently throughout Acts.

[4] Stendahl, PCB, p. 787. Cf. Bornkamm,"Der Auferstandene . . .," p. 184.

[5] There is a partial parallel in Lk. 17:3, but a "Q" origin of the pericope appears unlikely. See G. Barth, TIM, p. 84.

correction backed up by evidence from one or two witnesses (v. 16) both fail, then the matter must be brought before the whole community (ἐκκλησία) with excommunication as the final step if even a communal reprimand fails (v. 17). This detailed procedure is followed in v. 18 by a repetition of the words about binding and loosing (cp. 16:19), but this time addressed to the community as a whole.[1]

We conclude, then, that the stress on the regulation of the community in 16:18f. and 18:15-17 also has a counterpart in the final verses of the Gospel: disciples are to be initiated into the ἐκκλησία by baptism and then taught to observe the commands of Jesus which are the substance of the community's life.[2]

H. The Command to Teach (28:20a)

Besides baptizing, the eleven -- as we have seen -- are to make new disciples by teaching them to observe all that Jesus had enjoined during his ministry. The text suggests that the instruction envisaged here is post-baptismal, a practice well known during the apostolic period.[3]

---

[1] F. Beare, The Earliest Records of Jesus (New York, 1962), p. 151.

[2] For complete discussions of Matthean ecclesiology, see Stendahl, School; Bornkamm, "End-Expectation and Church in Matthew," TIM, pp. 38ff., and "Der Auferstandene . . .," pp. 183-88; Trilling, esp. pp. 143-63.

[3] See Acts 2:37-42, 8:12f., 9:18f., 10:34-48, 16:13-15, 18:8-11; cf. Dodd, "The Primitive Catechism and the Sayings of Jesus," in Dodd, More New Testament Studies (Grand Rapids, Michigan; 1968), pp. 11-29.

Although Matthew reproduces just seven of Mark's seventeen
uses of διδάσκω,[1] he alters Mark's "preaching in their synagogues"
(1:39) to read "teaching in their synagogues and preaching the gospel
of the kingdom" (4:23, cp. 9:35). He also adds to his source the summary statement that, after instructing the twelve, Jesus went on "to
teach (διδάσκειν) and preach in their cities" (11:1). More significantly, Matthew begins the Sermon on the Mount with, "And he opened his
mouth and taught (ἐδίδασκεν) them . . ." (5:2, no. par. in Lk.).
Referring to the law a few verses later, Jesus states: "whoever then
relaxes one of the least of these commandments[2] and teaches (διδάξῃ)
men so, shall be called least in the kingdom of heaven; but he who does
them and teaches (διδάξῃ) them shall be called great in the kingdom
of heaven" (5:19, no par.). The Sermon ends with the summary statement,
"and when Jesus finished these sayings, the crowds were astonished at
his teaching (διδαχῇ), for he taught (διδάσκων) them as one who
had authority (ἐξουσίαν), and not as their scribes" (7:28-29, cp.
Mk. 1:21-22). Since the Sermon represents an important example of Jesus'
teaching, the use of διδάσκω is not surprising. Its use in the
Gospel's conclusion is another indication of how Matthew pulls principal

---

[1]Stendahl, School (p. 22, n. 3), after noting this, adds: "The terms
of the διδάσκειν are used in a very distinct way by Matthew and the
teaching is considered the task of the disciples, 5:19, 28:20; cf. 10:25,
23:8. In Mark there is no explicit command to teach, though it is taken
for granted, Mk. 6:30."

[2]ἐντολῶν; cp. the related verb ἐνετειλάμην in 28:20 where it
is related, as here, to a form of διδάσκω.

themes together to shape the commissioning. The disciples must teach, just as Jesus had.

In the story of the rich young man, Matthew has edited Mark to produce an expression resembling ". . . to observe (τηρεῖν) all that I have commanded (ἐνετειλάμην) you" (28:20a); "If you would enter life, keep (τήρει) the commandments" (τὰς ἐντολάς, 19:17). This points to the Matthean origin of the expression in 28:20a.[1] The verb "command" (ἐντέλλομαι) is not common in the NT. Here alone (28:20) in the Synoptic Gospels it is related to the content of all that Jesus has said to the disciples: "all that I have commanded you."[2]

In the Conclusion of Chapter Two, we pointed out that in five of the twenty-seven HB commissions studied the observance of all that God has commanded is mentioned. In four of these instances, the wording in the LXX is similar to that in Mt. 28:20 which has τήρειν πάντα ὅσα ἐνετειλάμην ὑμῖν ("to observe all that I have commanded you"):

Ex. 7:2   "But you Moses shall say to him Pharaoh __all that I__ command you (πάντα, ὅσα σοι ἐντέλλομαι)."

Jos. 1:7   "to observe and do as Moses my servant __commanded__ (ἐνετείλατό) __you__."[3]

---

[1]Cf. Strecker, __Weg__, p. 209, n. 7. Note also the use of τηρέω in Mt. 23:3 (no par.).

[2]G. Schrenk, "'Εντέλλομαι," __TDNT__, II, p. 545. At 17:9 Matthew has changed Mark's διεστείλατο (charged, 9:9) to ἐνετείλατο (commanded).

[3]MT is closer to Mt. here than LXX: ". . . being careful to do __accord-ing to all the law__ (k^e kol-hattôrah) which Moses my servant commanded you."

1 Chr. 22:13   "Then you will prosper if you are careful to do the
                ordinances and decisions which the Lord <u>commanded</u>
                (ἐνετείλατο) Moses for Israel."

Jer. 1:7   "and <u>whatever I command you</u> (καὶ κατὰ πάντα,
                ὅσα ἐὰν ἐντείλωμαί σοι), you shall
                speak" (cp. Jer. 1:17).[1]

    In light of the mention of Moses in three of the four quota-

tions above, the following observation is not surprising:

> This phrase [28:20a] echoes Matthew's habitual
> presentation of Jesus as the new Moses of a new
> Israel. The word 'command' does not affirm the
> establishment of a new Law, but of a new way of
> life, just as the Law of Moses established a way
> of life.[2]

The new Moses theme, like the others in the concluding verses of Matthew,

can be seen in several places. (1) In the infancy account, Jesus' escape

from Herod's execution order (2:13-20) resembles Moses' being placed in

a basket on the river's edge to avoid Pharaoh's execution order. Both

Moses and Jesus (through Joseph) are told by the Lord (or his messenger)

that they can safely return from exile (Jesus from Egypt, Moses from

Midian), and the reason is identical: "for all the men who were seeking

your life are dead. So Moses took his wife and his sons and set them on

an ass, and went back to the land of Egypt . . ." (Ex. 4:20f.) -- "for

---

[1]Trilling (p. 91), cites several other examples resembling 28:20: Ex.
29:35; Dt. 1:3, 41; 7:11; 12:11, 14; 2 Chron. 33:8.

[2]McKenzie, <u>JBC</u>, II, p. 114. See the similar opinion of J. Rohde,
<u>Rediscovering the Teaching of the Evangelists</u> (ET: Philadelphia, 1968),
p. 63; and Stendahl (<u>PCB</u>, p. 790). The latter adds that the new Moses
category is, at the same time, "greatly transcended," so that "commandments" may include the keeping of the eucharistic meal (26:26-8) and the
orders of church discipline (18:15-22).

those[1] who sought the child's life are dead. And he rose and took the child and his mother and went to the land of Israel" (Mt. 2:20-21).

Also the coming of Jesus out of Egypt is explicitly paralleled with the Exodus under Moses and viewed as fulfilling prophecy (Mt. 2:15).[2]

(2) Matthew has added to the "forty days" in the desert -- mentioned in Mk. 1:13 and Lk. 4:2 -- "and forty nights" (Mt. 4:2), so that a clearer parallel to Moses' experience on Mt. Sinai is presented (Ex. 34:28, Dt. 9:9, 11, 18). (3) Matthew adds a descriptive detail to the Markan Transfiguration account which alludes to Moses. After the words, "and he was transfigured before them" (Mk. 9:2), Matthew inserts: "and his face shone like the sun" (17:2). The allusion is to Ex. 35:29-35 which describes how Moses' face shone because he had been on Mt. Sinai talking with God.[3] The transfiguration account goes on to mention that Jesus conversed with Moses and Elijah (Mk. 9:4, Mt. 17:3). While discussing 28:16, we mentioned Matthew's use of the mountain as the place of

---

[1]W. D. Davies, The Setting of the Sermon on the Mount (Cambridge, 1964), p. 78, points out the use of the plural, "those who sought . . . are dead" (οἱ ζητοῦντες . . . τεθνήκασιν), even though Herod alone has died (2:19). This strengthens the view that the Matthean text is modelled on that in Exodus 4.

[2]Blair, pp. 133f. Regarding the history of the tradition behind Mt. 2, Bultmann (HST, pp. 293f.) thinks that Matthew found the story of the flight into Egypt and the return (vv. 13-23) in his source "in some form." However, the literary shaping of this pericope and of the entire chapter is the work of Matthew. Davies goes further, and considers Mt. 1-2 "a unity wrought by the Evangelist" (p. 62) which allows us to look for possible themes governing their contents. So it appears that we are justified in identifying Matthean motifs in Ch. 2.

[3]Grundmann, Matthäus, p. 403.

revelation. Again a parallel to Moses' Sinaitic revelation may be
intended.[1] The revelatory mountain theme is most explicit in the
Sermon on the Mount (5:1ff.) where Jesus is cast as a second Moses who
presents a new message which aims at a deepening of the Mosaic Torah.[2]

Despite the presence of this material linking Jesus to Moses,
caution is necessary so as not to exaggerate its implications. Although
Matthew was aware of and alluded to the idea that Jesus' prototype was
Moses (as our survey has shown), he does not strongly emphasize it.
Rather, he pictures Jesus not as Moses who has come as Messiah, but as
Messiah, Son of Man, Emmanuel who has absorbed the Mosaic function.[3]
The caveat certainly applies to 28:16-20 where we have allusions to
Moses, but where the thought of Jesus as the Messianic teacher (28:20a)
predominates.

I. The Significance of the Adjective "All"

The adjective πᾶς (all) occurs four times in vv. 18b-20[4] and
thus tends to tie the verses together stylistically. (1) Jesus is the

---

[1]So, cautiously, Davies, p. 85.

[2]See, esp., 5:17-20. G. Barth, TIM, pp. 69, 157-58. "The reminder of the
mount on which the law was given means rather that here the right interpretation of the Sinai law is provided" (157). "Hence the Moses typology can
only be intended to confirm the teaching of Jesus as genuine teaching from
Sinai" (158). Apropos of this discussion is the following quotation from
Exodus Rabbah 12(75a) (which refers to Ex. 7-12, the plagues of Egypt)
cited in P. Billerbeck, Kommentar zum Neuen Testament aus Talmud und
Midrash, V. I, Das Evangelium nach Matthäus (Munich, 1922), p. 1054: "For
Moses thus had authority on earth and in heaven" (cp. Mt. 28:18; italics
mine).

[3]Davies, pp. 92f.

[4]Cp. the similar use of πᾶς elsewhere in Matthew: 3:15, 5:18, 7:12,
23:3. Still, there is nothing else in Matthew comparable to the emphatic
use of πᾶς four times in these two and one half verses.

recipient of all authority (πᾶσα ἐξουσία); (2) he wants the

eleven to make disciples of all nations (πάντα τὰ ἔθνη), and

(3) to teach them to observe all (πάντα ὅσα) that he has commanded;

(4) he promises to remain with them all days (πάσας τὰς ἡμέρας).

In Chapter Two the prevalence of "all" (Heb. kōl) in commissionings was

discussed.[1] Matthew once again appears to be influenced by a charac-

teristic term from the commissioning tradition. The fourfold use of

πᾶς in 28:18-20 further emphasizes the extent and significance of the

commission.

J. The Word of Assurance (28:20b)

1. "And lo (behold), I . . ." (καὶ ἰδοὺ ἐγὼ)

This expression is sometimes used in HB commissions,[2] but

often elsewhere in the HB. The simple ἰδού or καὶ ἰδού (not

followed by ἐγώ) is used often throughout the First Gospel.[3] "Behold,

I . . ." is employed occasionally.[4] Since Luke also uses "and behold,

I . . ." in his version of the Easter commission,[5] we must be careful

not to exaggerate the significance of it in Matthew. Both Gospels may

have been influenced by a prevalent HB expression.

---

[1]P. 40, n. 1; p. 66, n. 3.

[2]See above, pp. 54f. "Behold, I . . ." occurs in seven of the twenty-
seven HB pericopes studied.

[3]E.g., in the resurrection narrative: 28:2, 7, 9, 11 (contrast its complete absence from Mk. 16:1-8); in the infancy narrative: 1:20, 23
(quoted from Is. 7:14); 2:1, 9, 13, 19.

[4]10:16, 28:7 (pronoun "I" contained in verb in this case only), 28:20.

[5]Luke also uses "behold" frequently. See below, p. 119, n. 2.

2. "I am with you . . ."

In 28:20 "and behold" is joined to the expression of REASS
". . . I am with you always, to the close of the age." "Behold I am
(my covenant is) with you" is found in two HB commissionings (Gen. 17:4,
28:15), and the simple "I am (will be) with you" or an equivalent expression occurs in another thirteen of the twenty-seven pericopes, sometimes
more than once.[1] Thus, more than half of the HB pericopes employ the
specific expression of reassurance via divine presence which is found in
Mt. 28:20. Jesus is there pictured as giving to his disciples the same
reassurance through his active, dynamic presence that God is pictured as
giving in the HB: ἐγὼ μεθ' ὑμῶν εἰμι (28:20).[2] The phrase
is also a fulfillment of the interpretation of Jesus' mission provided
by Matthew via the "formula" quotation from Is. 7:14: ". . . and his
name shall be called Immanuel." To this Matthew adds, "which means,
God with us" μεθ' ἡμῶν ὁ θεός (1:23). Thus the beginning and end
of the Gospel are linked by the "God-with-us" theme, which is extremely
widespread not only in commissionings, as seen, but in the HB generally.[3]
Matthew, influenced by the preponderance of the theme, has incorporated
it into his Gospel at these two points, both of which are redactional.

---

[1] See above, p. 66, n. 1.

[2] P. Fiedler, Die Formel "und Siehe" im Neuen Testament (Munich, 1969),
p. 52.

[3] E.g., Gen. 21:20; Dt. 20:1, 4; 31:6, 8; Jos. 1:17; 2 Sam. 7:3; Is. 41:10;
43:2, 5; Hag. 1:13.

The "Emmanuel" passage (1:22f.) is the first of the eleven Matthean "formula" quotations.[1] He has inserted vv. 22f. into material known to him from tradition which narrated the birth of Jesus.[2] As we have demonstrated in Chapter Four,[3] 28:20b represents a redaction of the common commissioning tradition in which Jesus reassures the disciples by promising to send the Holy Spirit. The "God-with-us" theme in 1:23 and 28:20 is also found in a variant form in 18:20 where Jesus states that "where two or three are gathered in my name, there I am in the midst of them." Jesus' presence in the congregation is here described as analogous to the Shekhinah or presence of God.[4] The place of the Torah is taken by the "name" of Jesus, the Shekhinah by Jesus himself.[5]

3. "... always to the close of the age."

"Always" translates the Gk. πάσας τὰς ἡμέρας (lit., "all days"). Found only here in the NT, it helps to specify the duration

---

[1] Cf. Stendahl, PCB, p. 770.

[2] Bultmann, HST, p. 291.

[3] Pp. 117f.

[4] Cf. Pirke Aboth 3,2: "But, when two sit and there are between them words of Torah, the Shekhinah rests between them . . ." R. Travers Herford (trans.) The Ethics of the Talmud: Sayings of the Fathers (New York, 1945). Trilling (p. 41) cites numerous examples from Deuteronomy which form the background for the later rabbinic view of the Shekhinah. They all speak of the "place where the Lord will choose to make his name dwell." See Dt. 12:11; 14:23; 16:2, 6, 11; 26:2.

[5] G. Barth, TIM, p. 135.

of Jesus' presence. However, it is the characteristically Matthean[1]
ἕως τῆς συντελείας τοῦ αἰῶνος which most fully conveys
the enduring presence of the risen Jesus. The phrase gives no hint of
how near or how far away the close of the age will be.[2] It points to
the strong faith of the Church in the continual presence of the risen
Christ rather than to apocalyptic speculation.

III. Conclusions

(a) As several scholars have argued, 28:16(18)-20 is a summary of the entire Gospel.[3] The following themes or ideas from the body
of the work are recapitulated in its concluding verses: the mountain as
a place of revelation (v. 16); the need for faith (v. 17); the authority
of Jesus (v. 18); the importance of discipleship (v. 19a); the universalistic emphasis (v. 19a); the need to order the community (here, by
means of baptism and teaching; [vv. 19b-20a]); Jesus as a new Moses
(20a); Jesus' enduring presence (20b).

---

[1]The expression, "the close of the age," is employed, with one exception
(Heb. 9:26), only by Matthew in the NT. In Hebrews the expression is
used in a different sense to describe Christ's coming "at the end of
the age" (= the time of the historical Jesus) to atone for sin. Matthew
also uses the phrase in 13:39, 40, 49 and 24:3.

[2]Lohmeyer, Matthäus, p. 422; Trilling, p. 45. He notes that the parables
of the wicked servant (24:45-51) and of the ten virgins (25:1-13) urge
preparedness for the end whenever it comes. As further proof that the
delay of the parousia was not an issue in the Matthean church, Trilling
notes its absence in the rest of the gospel and the fact that sayings
about the imminent expectation (10:23, 16:28) are retained without
significant alteration (pp. 44-5). Cf. Stendahl, PCB, p. 798.

[3]E.g., Michel, "Der Abschluss . . .," p. 21; Trilling, p. 21; Blair,
pp. 45-6; G. Schille, "Das Evangelium des Matthäus als Katechismus,"
NTS 4 (1957/8), 113.

(b) The question of the history of the tradition behind 28:16-20 can be answered only after the Easter commissioning accounts in the other Gospels are compared with the Matthean account and the shape of the common tradition underlying them all is set forth in Chapter Four. However, it should be clear from the foregoing analysis that Matthew has shaped his version of the tradition in language characteristic of his Gospel. Thus, the following words or expressions were shown to be Matthean: "worshipped," "doubted," "came and said to them," "in heaven and on earth," "therefore," "make disciples," "teaching" and "to the close of the age."

(c) The concluding verses are modeled on the HB commissioning Gattung. They contain an INT (v. 16), a CONF (17a and 18), a REAC (17b), a COMM (19-20a) and a REASS (20b). Expressions typical of HB commissionings are also reflected there: "go," "command," "I am with you" and the fourfold use of the adjective "all."

Chapter Four THE MATTHEAN REDACTION OF A

PRIMITIVE APOSTOLIC COMMISSIONING

I. Introduction

We will now attempt to answer two of the most central questions

of the entire study: (1) Did Matthew base his version of Jesus' post-

resurrection commissioning on a common tradition about it which was also

known to Luke, John and perhaps to the author of the longer ending of

Mark (16:9-20)?[1] (2) If so, how did he redact or edit it? Several

scholars accept the thesis of a common tradition which lies behind Mt.

28:16-20, Lk. 24:36-49, Jn. 20:19-23 and, with some exceptions, Ps.-Mk.

16:14-18.[2]

Since the question of whether or not any material in Pseudo-

Mark is independent of the other Gospels is difficult to answer, we will

---

[1]As we shall see when studying this pericope, there is widespread scholarly agreement that it was composed by someone other than Mark. Therefore, it will be described hereafter as "Pseudo-Mark" (abbrev., "Ps.-Mk.").

[2]R. Brown, The Gospel according to John, XII-XXI, Anchor Bible V. 29A
(hereafter, "John 29A") (Garden City, N.Y.; 1970), pp. 972, 1027-31; R.
Bultmann, The Gospel of John (ET: Philadelphia, 1971), p. 690; C. H.
Dodd, Historical Tradition in the Fourth Gospel (Cambridge, 1963), p.
144; G. Delling, "The Significance of the Resurrection of Jesus for Faith
in Jesus Christ," in book by same title ed. by C. F. D. Moule (Naperville,
Ill.; 1968), p. 92; C. F. Evans, Resurrection and the New Testament
(Naperville, Ill.; 1970), p. 130; Fuller, pp. 117f.; G. D. Kilpatrick,
The Origins of the Gospel According to St. Matthew (Oxford, 1946), p. 49;
W. Marxsen, The Resurrection of Jesus of Nazareth (ET: Philadelphia,
1970), pp. 79f. Bultmann, Kilpatrick and Marxsen do not include Pseudo-
Mark.

not base conclusions on the evidence therein. The more traditional conclusion has been that Pseudo-Mark is a second century (or third century) creation based on material in the other Gospels and in Acts.[1] As we have indicated, however, some scholars[2] think that the Pseudo-Markan commission itself (vv. 14-18) is independent of the other Gospels. We agree in part, and have attempted to show why in Appendix One. For the present, however, Ps.-Mk. 16:14-18 will be brought in only to corroborate conclusions which appear to follow from an analysis of the post-resurrection commissionings in Matthew, Luke and John.

II. Evidence of a Common Tradition

So as to make clear the parallel elements in the commissionings, they are presented together below. Pseudo-Mark is included to enable the reader to evaluate better the question of whether or not it contains independent material.

A. Schematization of Commissionings (next page)

B. An Analysis of the Schematization

(1) All four accounts exhibit most of the elements of the commission Gattung. Only Pseudo-Mark lacks a REAC. There is no CONC in Matthew and John, but we have attempted to explain why.[3] The PROT is missing in all four, but this is not surprising since most HB commissionings have either a PROT or a REAC.

---

[1]See, e.g., Beare, p. 246; F. C. Grant, "Mark, Exegesis," IB, 7, p. 915; R. McL. Wilson, "Mark," PCB, p. 819.

[2]See p. 98, n. 2.

[3]P. 101, n. 1.

A. Schematization of Commissionings

	Matthew 28:16-20	Pseudo-Mark 16:14-20	Luke 24:36-53	John 20:19-23
INT	The eleven disciples went to appointed mountain in Galilee.	The eleven were sitting at table.	Emmaus disciples were discussing their experience with the eleven (v. 33) on Sunday evening.	Disciples were gathered on Sunday evening behind locked doors for fear of Jews.
CONF	Jesus approached and spoke to them. All authority . . .	Jesus appeared and upbraided them for their lack of faith.	Jesus stood among them (ἔστη ἐν μέσῳ αὐτῶν)	Jesus came and stood among them (ἔστη εἰς τὸ μέσον)
REAC	Seeing him (ἰδόντες αὐτὸν) they worshipped him, but some doubted.		They were startled and frightened, and supposed that they saw a spirit (v. 37) . . . while they still disbelieved for joy (ἀπὸ τῆς χαρᾶς) and wondered (v. 41) . . .	The disciples were glad (ἐχάρησαν) when they saw (ἰδόντες) the Lord.
COMM	Go (πορευθέντες) and make disciples of all nations (πάντα τὰ ἔθνη), baptizing them in the name (ὄνομα) of the Father and of the Son and of the Holy Spirit.	Go (πορευθέντες) into all (ἅπαντα) the world and preach (κηρύξατε) to the whole (πάσῃ) creation. He who believes and is baptized will be saved . . .	. . . repentence and forgiveness (ἄφεσιν) of sins should be preached (κηρυχθῆναι) in his name (ὀνόματι) to all nations (πάντα τὰ ἔθνη) (v. 47).	As the Father has sent (ἀπέσταλκέν) me, so I send you . . . Receive the Holy Spirit. If you forgive (ἀφῆτε) the sins of any, they are forgiven . . . retained.

REASS	And behold, I (καὶ ἰδοὺ ἐγὼ) am with you always (πάσας τὰς ἡμέρας) . . .	These signs will accompany those who believe: in my name (ὀνόματι) they will cast out demons . . .	Why are you troubled . . . See (ἴδετε) my hands and my feet, that it is I myself . . . Have you anything here to eat? . . . He took a piece of broiled fish and ate before them. (vv. 38-42) . . . and behold, I (καὶ ἰδοὺ ἐγὼ) send (ἐξαποστέλλω) the promise of my Father upon you; but stay in city until clothed with power.	Peace to you . . . he showed them his hands and his side . . . (v. 19b).
CONC[1]		Jesus taken up into heaven. Disciples go forth and preach (ἐκήρυξαν) everywhere (πανταχοῦ) while Lord worked with them (συνεργοῦντος) and confirmed message by signs.	Jesus parted from disciples at Bethany. They returned to Jerusalem with great joy (χαρᾶς) and were continually in temple blessing God.	

---

[1] We have already explained the reasons for the lack of a CONC in Matthew (Ch. 3, pp. 69f.). The absence of a CONC in John is explained by Brown (John 29A, p. 1051) in a way which resembles our explanation for the lack of one in Matthew: "It is fitting that the last words in the original Johannine Gospel [20:29] are words of Jesus -- who is not said to have departed . . . . He remains present [cp. Mt. 28:20] in the Paraclete/Spirit who is to be with the disciples forever (Jn. 16:19)."

(2) There are several verbal and thematic parallels. Here
we will mention only those which apply to Matthew, Luke and John.
Parallels between Pseudo-Mark and the other Gospels will be discussed
in Appendix One.

a. Matthew-Luke: The identical expression καὶ ἰδοὺ ἐγὼ
("and behold, I . . ."); the express mention of the "eleven" disciples:[1]
the authoritative character of Jesus' name; the universal mission
(πάντα τὰ ἔθνη, "all nations", appears in both); the theme of
disbelief.[2] There may also be a parallel between the use of ἐξουσία
("authority", Mt. 28:18) and δύναμιν ("power", Lk. 24:49): Jesus'
possession of universal authority is what empowers the disciples in
Matthew, just as the Spirit will clothe them with power in Luke.[3]

b. Luke-John: The Jerusalem venue; Christophany occurring
on Sunday evening (see Lk. 24:13, 33); Jesus described as coming with a
certain suddenness and "standing among them;"[4] the apologetic proof-
motif whereby Jesus physically demonstrates that it is he and not a

---

[1]The "eleven . . . and those who were with them" are mentioned in Lk.
24:33 just before the Christophany (vv. 36-49).

[2]Brown, John 29A (p. 1032) comments that the theme of disbelief is found
in Mt. 28:17, Ps.-Mk. 16:14, Lk. 24:37-41. He proposes that in John the
statement, "He showed them his hands and his side" was originally preceded by an expression of doubt (cp. Lk. 24:37-9), but that the evangelist has transferred it to a separate episode (20:24-9) and personified
it in Thomas. Cp. Bultmann, John, p. 691. Dodd, "The Appearances . . .",
p. 12, comments: ". . . the Lord 'showed them his hands and his side,'
[Jn. 20:20] thus setting at rest, by proof tendered, a doubt which was
there though unexpressed."

[3]It is probably not coincidental that Luke, in the sending out of the
twelve (9:1), redacts Mark's, ". . . and gave them authority (ἐξουσίαν)
over unclean spirits," (6:7) to, ". . . and gave them power (δύναμιν)
and authority over all demons." (Matthew, 10:1, simply has "authority.")

[4]Brown, John 29A, p. 1028.

ghost; the mention of the disciples' joy; the motif of sending ([ἐξ]

ἀποστέλλω); the words about forgiveness of sins;[1] the giving of the

spirit to the disciples by Jesus (Lk.-"... I send the promise of my

Father [i.e., the Holy Spirit] upon you ..." Jn.-"Receive the Holy

Spirit ...").

    c. Matthew-Luke-John: the use of a second aorist form of

the verb ὁράω (εἶδον, see) in connection with the disciples'

encounter with Jesus (Mt.-"When they saw him ..." Lk.-"See my hands

and my feet ... handle me and see ..." Jn.-"disciples were glad

when they saw the Lord"); the express mention of God "the Father;"

the commission to spread Jesus' message; the theme of continual divine

presence (Mt.-"with you always;" Lk.-"I send the promise of my Father

[the Holy Spirit] upon you;" Jn.-"receive the Holy Spirit;"[2] a reference

of some kind to the Holy Spirit (Mt.-"baptizing them in the name of ...

---

[1]Both Gospels mention the forgiveness of sins (Jn. 20:23; Lk. 24:47).
John specifically refers to the sending of the disciples (v. 21) and the
giving of the Holy Spirit (22) before the mention of forgiveness. The
Lucan references are subtler: "forgiveness of sins should be preached
in his name to all nations" (24:47), and "the promise of my Father" (49).
Brown, John 29A, pp. 1028f.

[2]The Spirit makes divine presence possible. Cp. Jn. 14:16f.: "... he
[the Father] will give you another counselor to be with you forever
[μεθ' ὑμῶν εἰς τὸν αἰῶνα; cp. Mt. 28:20] even the Spirit
of truth." Brown, John 29A, p. 644 comments on 14:16f.: "The Old Testament theme of 'God with us' (the Immanuel of Is. 7:14) is now to be
realized in the Paraclete/Spirit who remains with the disciples forever".
Dodd, "The Appearances ...," p. 17, sees the theme of divine presence
in Lk. 24:49, Mt. 28:20 and Jn. 20:22f.

the Holy Spirit;" Lk.-"behold, I send the promise of my Father upon you
. . . clothed with power from on high;" Jn.-"receive the Holy Spirit").[1]

These comparisons indicate the greatest disparity between
Matthew and John and the greatest similarity between Luke and John.[2]
Yet the affinities between Luke and Matthew indicate that Luke stands
between the other two Gospels, though closer to John.

III. An Exegesis of the Lukan and Johannine Commissionings

No attempt will be made to answer every exegetical question
relating to Lk. 24:36-53 and Jn. 20:19-23, but only those having a direct
bearing on the question at hand: did a common or proto-commissioning
constitute the basis of the commissioning accounts in Luke, John and,
most importantly, Matthew?

---

[1]"The most one may argue from these late references to the Holy Spirit
[Mt. 28:19, Lk. 24:49, Jn. 20:22] is that the early tradition of the
appearance may have contined a reference to an outpouring of the Spirit
. . . a reference that the various Gospels adapted in different ways."
Brown, John 29A, p. 1030.

[2]Brown, John 29A, p. 1028, views the two accounts (Luke and John) as
"probably independent versions of the original Jerusalem narrative of
the appearance of Jesus to his disciples." However, he also considers
that one basic appearance underlies all the main Gospel accounts of
appearances to the twelve (eleven) regardless of the time or place the
appearances are put by the Evangelists (ibid., p. 972). More will be
said on this in the discussion of the original (proto-) commissioning
narrative below. Cf. Bultmann, John, p. 690 whose position resembles
Brown's.

A.   Luke 24:36-53

<u>INT</u>:   (36a "As they were saying this . . .")

The location of the encounter is Jerusalem (cp. Jn. 20:19-23) which is consistent with the theological significance of the city in Luke.[1]

<u>CONF</u>:   (36b ". . . Jesus himself stood among them.")

<u>REAC</u>:   (37,41). The sudden Christophany startled and frightened the disciples (v. 37). Even after Jesus shows them his hands and his feet, they cannot quite believe their own eyes:[2] ". . . they still disbelieved for joy and wondered."

<u>REASS</u>:   (38-42, 49). Jesus provides tangible proof that it is he by inviting the disciples to touch him and by eating broiled fish in their presence.

The aspect of the REASS corresponding most closely to Matthew and representing the Lucan version of the motif of divine presence occurs in v. 49. Matthew's "and behold, I am with you always . . ." has as its counterpart Lk. 24:49a, "and behold, I send the promise of my Father upon you." These words express the promise of the outpouring of the Spirit described in Acts 2 (cp., esp. 2:33). The disciples will be "clothed with power" (Lk. 24:49) by the Spirit. This endowment with power is the

---

[1]"Jerusalem is the scene where redemptive history is fulfilled." H. Flender, <u>St. Luke: Theologian of Redemptive History</u> (ET: New York, 1967), p. 107. See H. Conzelmann, <u>The Theology of St. Luke</u> (ET: New York, 1960), p. 213.

[2]E. E. Ellis, <u>The Gospel of Luke</u> (London, 1966), p. 279.

result of the Holy Spirit's presence[1] which is the Lukan equivalent of
Jesus' enduring presence (Mt. 28:20).

COMM: (44-48). As noted earlier, the Lukan commission is less direct
than those in the other Gospels; but it certainly qualifies as one.
Vv. 44-46 set the stage by Jesus' justifying scripturally his suffering,
death and resurrection. V. 47 speaks of the actual mission: the preaching of "repentence and [lit., 'unto'] forgiveness of sins" to all nations
(πάντα τὰ ἔθνη, exactly as in Mt. 28:19). "You are witnesses to
these things" is "at the same time a commission and a· statement of fact."[2]
The indirectness of the commission is dictated by Luke's theology of
history. In contrast to John, and Matthew, he stresses the era of the
Church as a distinct phase of redemptive history not beginning until
Pentecost. The disciples are to wait in Jerusalem until (ἕως)
are "clothed with power from on high" (24:49).[3] John, on the other hand,
reports that Jesus commissioned the disciples through the reception of
the Spirit on Easter Sunday evening (20:19-23). Similarly, Matthew describes Jesus as commissioning the eleven to begin their work immediately
equipped with his authority and abiding presence (28:18-20).

---

[1]Cf. Conzelmann, p. 204.

[2]J. Schmid, Das Evangelium nach Lukas (Regensburg, 1960), p. 362. He
adds: "This word of Jesus [v. 48] corresponds to the trinitarian
missionary and baptismal command in Mt. 28:19-20. Cp. G. W. H. Lampe,
"Luke," PCB, p. 842; Grundmann, Das Evangelium nach Lukas (Theologischer
Handkommentar zum Neuen Testament) (Berlin, 1961), p. 453.

[3]Cf. Conzelmann, pp. 135-6, 204, 206.

CONC: (50-53).[1] Jesus blesses the disciples and then "parts from them"

at Bethany. The disciples return joyfully to Jerusalem to praise God

---

[1]Conzelmann (p. 203, n. 4) thinks vv. 50-3 may be a later interpolation
because they present a rival account of the Ascension with the non-
Lucan setting in Bethany and the lack of any delimitation of the period
of the appearances (contrast Acts 1:3, 13:31). P. Menoud in "Remarques
sur les textes de l'Ascension dans Luc-Actes," Neutestamentliche Studien
für R. Bultmann, W. Eltester (ed.) (Berlin, 1954), pp. 148-56, wants to
eliminate both Lk. 24:50-3 and Acts 1:1-5 as later interpolations. He
feels that Lk. 24:50-3 is composed on the basis of Acts 1:6-14. He notes
that the expression "lifting up his hands" is used only here in the NT
but is common in the Church Fathers after the second century. Also the
expression, "with great joy" (24:52) is entirely unmotivated in its
present context but explicable on the basis of Acts 1:9-11 where the
"two men" assure the disciples that Jesus "will come in the same way as
you saw him go into heaven." Cp. A. Wilder, "Variant Traditions of the
Resurrection in Acts," JBL 62 (1943), 306-11. Against these opinions,
we would argue that Lk. 24:50-3 is integral to the structure of the
Gospel because it thus begins at the temple (1:5ff.) and ends there. In
each case there is a priestly action (Zechariah's burning of incense,
1:8-9; Jesus' blessing of the disciples, 24:50). Moreover, a redactor
would hardly have introduced the discrepancy between Jesus' having as-
cended on Easter (or the following day, 24:50-3) or forty days later
(Acts 1:3). The discrepancy can be explained if the forty days is inter-
preted symbolically (P. A. van Stampvoort, "The Interpretation of the
Ascension in Luke and Acts," NTS 5 [1958-59], 30-42; Cf. Grundmann,
Lukas, p. 454). Flender (p. 12) justifies both accounts on the basis of
the different slant which each gives to the translation of Jesus from
life on earth to life in heaven. Lk. 24:50-3 concentrates on the "human
angle": the disciples receive Jesus' blessing, he parts from them and
they return joyfully to Jerusalem and praise God in the temple. Acts
1:9-11 looks at the event "from above, in the light of the destiny of
the Lord of heaven." The word οὐρανός ("heaven") is used four times
here and not at all in Lk. 24:50-3 (unless 51b is considered genuine;
see below).

Without the clause, "and was carried up into heaven" (51b--omitted
both in the Nestle text and RSV on the basis of its absence from Codex
Sinaiticus and Codex Bezae), Lk. 24:51a still alludes to the Ascension
in the expression, "he parted from them" (Schmid, Lukas, p. 363; cp.
Marxsen, Resurrection, p. 54). Some scholars, however, consider 51b
authentic on the basis of its presence in Alexandrinus, Vaticanus,
Ephraemi, Washington and elsewhere and because the later interpolation
of 51b would create further difficulties vis-a-vis Acts 1. See Fuller,
p. 122; C. Stuhlmueller, "Luke," JBC, I, p. 163; Grundmann, Lukas, p. 454,
n. 24.

in the temple. Stylistically vv. 50-53 are interlocked with 36-49 as
if they treated of the same Easter day.[1]

B. John 20:19-23

INT: (19a). The INT is typical since it describes the disciples' situation: they are gathered behind closed doors on Sunday evening.

CONF: (19b). ". . . Jesus came and stood among them and said to them,
'Peace be with you.'" There is a strongly epiphanic note to Jesus'
appearance: he stands suddenly in the midst of the disciples even
though the doors are locked. He then greets them with εἰρήνη ὑμῖν
(peace [be] to [with] you). In rabbinic Hebrew šālôm 'ᵃlᵉkem or lᵃkem
(peace [be] to [with] you) was a standard greeting.[2]

REASS: (20a). "When he had said this, he showed them his hands and his
side." The apologetic motif appears, though not as strongly as in Lk.
24:39-43.[3] This is probably explained by the strong apologetic motif in
the Thomas pericope which follows (20:24-9).

REAC: (20b). "Then the disciples were glad (ἐχάρησαν) when they
saw (ἰδόντες) the Lord." Keeping in mind that Jesus had just shown

---

[1] Stuhlmueller, JBC, II, p. 163.

[2] Brown, John 29A, p. 1021; Bultmann, John, p. 691. Dodd, as pointed out
pp. 12f., identifies the "greeting" as an element in the Gattung of
"concise" resurrection narratives distinct from what he calls "the
appearance of the Lord" ("The Appearances . . ., p. 11). We prefer to
subsume the greeting and the appearance under the CONF because only one
of the four commissionings under investigation here has a greeting
(Jn. 20:19).

[3] On the implicit element of doubt in John, see p. 102, n. 2.

the disciples "his hands and his side" (v. 20a), the following similarities to the Lukan account are noteworthy:

(a) See: "See (ἴδετε) my hands and my feet . . . handle
me and see (ἴδετε) . . ." (Lk. 24:39).

(b) Joy (gladness): "And while they still disbelieved for
joy (ἀπὸ τῆς χαρᾶς) . . ." (Lk. 24:41).[1]

COMM: (21-3). The first element in the COMM ("As the Father has sent
me . . . I send you") parallels Mt. 28:19 ("Go . . . make disciples of
all nations") and Lk. 24:47 (". . . repentance and forgiveness of sins
should be preached to all nations . . .").[2] Then the Spirit is imparted
by Jesus to the disciples who thus are empowered to continue Jesus'
judicial function in regard to evil by forgiving or retaining sins.[3]

The words about the disciples' authority to forgive (ἀφῆτε
. . . ἀφέωνται) sins and to retain them are paralleled by Lk. 24:47:
". . . repentance and forgiveness of sins (μετάνοιαν εἰς ἄφεσιν
ἁμαρτιῶν) should be preached . . ."

---

[1]In Matthew the motif of seeing is also present ("And when they saw him
. . .") and is also joined to a REAC on the disciples' part (". . . they
worshipped him; but some doubted," 28:17).

[2]Brown, John 29A, pp. 1029f. who also mentions Ps.-Mk. 16:15: "Go into
all the world and preach the Gospel to the whole creation." Bultmann
(John, p. 692) comments: "Doubtless the Evangelist's [John's] composition replaces a more original formulation of the source, which should
be thought of as perhaps analogous to Lk. 24:47 or Mt. 28:19f."

[3]B. Vawter, "The Gospel according to John," JBC, II, p. 464. See Jn.
3:19, 5:27, 9:39. Brown, John 29A, sees baptism as one of several
possible ways in which the Church could exercise its function of forgiving and retaining sins (pp. 1041-45).

IV. The Shape of the Common Tradition

Behind Matthew, Luke and John

We now intend to deduce what the proto-commissioning consisted
of from what has been learned in Parts II and III above.

A. The Appearance to the Eleven

In every account the eleven disciples are described as being
together. Only Jn. 20:19-23 does not explicitly mention the "eleven"
(ἔνδεκα). Yet 20:24 notes that "Thomas, one of the twelve . . . was
not with them when Jesus came." John has kept the traditional designation of twelve despite Judas.[1] It is difficult to tell from Jn. 20:19ff.
whether others besides the twelve (minus Thomas and Judas) were present.
Yet, in light of John's tendency to "enlarge the circle of apostles"
with such figures as Philip, Nathaniel, Lazarus, Thomas, Mary and
Martha and the Samaritan woman, it seems likely that others besides
the twelve were on hand.[2] Lk. 24:33 speaks of the eleven "and those who
were with them." Nevertheless, the eleven are important in the tradition.

Jesus then makes his appearance and is mentioned by name
(ὁ Ἰησοῦς) in Mt. 28:16 and Jn. 20:19.[3]

---

[1] Brown, John 29A, p. 1024.

[2] E. Käsemann, The Testament of Jesus (ET: London, 1968), p. 29.

[3] A variant reading in Lk. 24:36 adds ὁ Ἰησοῦς.

B. The Disciples' Reaction

We already noted the use of εἶδον (see) in each of the three commissionings and the way in which seeing Jesus is joined to the disciples' REAC of joy in Luke and John. To carry the analysis one step further, the REAC to seeing Jesus is a mixture of joy and doubt in Luke ("and while they still disbelieved for joy and wondered . . .," 24:44). It probably was the same at an earlier stage[1] in John, which now simply reads: "Then the disciples were glad when they saw the Lord" (20:20). In Matthew the disciple's REAC is a mixture of worship and doubt. Therefore, it appears that worship and joy are parallel ideas. Worship/joy, moreover, is juxtaposed to doubt/disbelief in each commissioning account (doubt implicit in John). We conclude then that the proto-commissioning contained some description both of a positive response to the Christophany and of a negative or disbelieving one.

C. The Commission

Words denoting mission are present in each Gospel:

1. Matthew- "Go, therefore, and make disciples of all nations . . ." (28:19).

2. Luke- ". . . repentance and forgiveness of sins should be preached to all nations, beginning from Jerusalem. You are witnesses of these things" (24:47f.).

3. John- "As the Father has sent me, even so I send you" (20:21).

---

[1]As explained above (p. 101, n. 1), the element of doubt in John has probably been transferred to the next pericope (Jn. 20:24-29, doubting Thomas). Note that after Jesus shows Thomas the wounds in his hands and side, his response is the worshipful, "My Lord and my God" (20:28).

The use by Matthew and Luke of the identical expression of universalism, "all nations" (πάντα τὰ ἔθνη) makes it probable that this was present in the proto-commission.[1] Bultmann maintains that the motif of a missionary charge of the risen Jesus (Mt. 28:16-20; Lk. 24:44-49; Acts 1:4-8; Jn. 20:19-23, 21:15-17) "is a quite late achievement of Hellenistic Christianity (if not also in part of Hellenist Jewish-Christianity)."[2] These accounts presuppose the universal mission as something enjoined by the risen One. Yet Gal. 2:7 indicates that the primitive Church knew nothing of this.[3] In Gal. 2 Paul discusses his controversy with Peter, James and John over the Gentile mission. He tells them that he has been entrusted with the gospel to the "uncircumcised" just as Peter has been entrusted with the gospel to the

---

[1] If Ps.-Mk. 16:15 is independent of the other Gospels, then the expression, "Go into all the world and preach the Gospel to the whole creation," would reinforce the view that the world-wide mission was part of the proto-commission. The absence of universalism in the Johannine commissioning might be explained by the Fourth Gospel's view of "the world" (ὁ κόσμος). Although in the first half of the Gospel there are references to Jesus' having been sent by the Father to save the world (3:17, 10:36, 12:47) and give life to it (6:33, 51), in the second half "the world" is quite consistently identified with those who have rejected Jesus under Satan's leadership. Jesus' coming has become a judgment on the world (9:39, 12:31), and he and his followers oppose and are hated by it (15:19; 16:33; 17:14, 16; 18:36). Brown, John I-XI, Anchor Bible V. 29 (Garden City, N.Y.; 1966), p. 509.

[2] HST, p. 289. Bultmann makes no comment whatever on Ps.-Mk. 16:9-20 in HST except a citation of 16:14 while discussing resurrection stories in which a meal plays a part (p. 291).

[3] Ibid., p. 289. Cp. V. Taylor, The Gospel according to St. Mark (New York, 1966²), p. 612, who cites the Apostolic Council (Acts 15) as proof that Jesus himself could not have initiated the Gentile mission.

"circumcised" (2:2, 7ff.). Paul's having to lay before them the gospel preached to the Gentiles would hardly have been necessary had Jesus actually commanded a Gentile mission. We agree with Bultmann that the universal missionary command is hardly *ipsissima verba Jesu*, an actual saying of Jesus. We disagree, though, with the characterization of the command as a "quite late achievement of Hellenistic Christianity." The Apostolic Council, discussed in Acts 15 and alluded to in Gal. 2, is generally agreed to have occurred ca. 48 C.E.[1] If Ogg[2] is correct in dating the crucifixion to the year 33, then within about fifteen years of Jesus' death and resurrection the Gentile mission had been firmly established by Paul and approved of by the "pillars" (Peter, James, John; Gal. 2:9). Furthermore, Dibelius[3] has shown that the story of the centurion Cornelius whom Peter was directed to associate with and to accept into the Christian community is not a Lucan invention. Though Luke has added a number of the details in the story (e.g., Peter's "Lucan" speech, 10:34-43), it goes back to an early tradition. This is confirmed by Gal. 2:11f. where Paul says that Peter, when he came to Antioch, "ate with the Gentiles" (though he changed his mind when members

---

[1]Fitzmyer, "The Letter to the Galatians," JBC, II, p. 239, argues for the identification of these two chapters with the same event. Cp. W. Kümmel, Introduction to the New Testament (ET: New York, 1966), p. 180; G. Ogg, "Chronology of the NT," PCB, p. 732. All accept a dating of ca. 48.

[2]Ibid., p. 730.

[3]Studies in the Acts of the Apostles (ET: London, 1956), pp. 109-22.

of James' party arrived).[1] Since the Cornelius episode occurred before
A.D. 48, the tradition of a universal missionary command probably originated even earlier (pace Bultmann).

Only John lacks a reference to the name of Jesus. However the
statement, "As the Father has sent me, even so I (κἀγὼ) send you
(20:21)" performs a similar function. Speaking in the first person, he
invests the disciples with the authority to carry forward his work
(v. 21) and to forgive and retain sins through reception of the Holy
Spirit (vv. 22f.) The Lucan account speaks of preaching in his name
(24:47) and the Matthean of baptism in the name of Father, Son and
Spirit, (28:19). In both cases ὄνομα relates to the power or authority vested in Jesus: power to preach repentance and forgiveness of
sins (Luke), or to baptize (Matthew).

Luke's COMM centers in Jesus' words that "repentance and
forgiveness of sins should be preached (κηρυχθῆναι) to all
nations . . ." (24:47). Matthew, as we saw,[2] uses the redactional verb,
μαθητεύσατε, in connection with the universal mission: "Go . . .
make disciples of all nations" (28:19). The sentence, though, could
have read: "Go . . . preach (the gospel)[3] to all nations, baptizing

---

[1]Hahn, Mission, p. 53.

[2]P. 82.

[3]Ps.-Mk. 16:15 reads: "Go into all the world and preach the gospel
to the whole creation." We will argue in Appendix 1 that this verse,
especially the clause, "preach the gospel to the whole creation," has
a high degree of probability of being an independent version of the
commissioning tradition.

them . . . teaching them to observe all that I have commanded you."
This is verified by a comparison of 28:19 with 10:7 (the sending out of
the twelve during Jesus' public ministry):

> "Go, therefore, and make disciples . . ."
> πορευθέντες οὖν μαθητεύσατε   (28:19)
> "And preach as you go . . ."
> πορευόμενοι δὲ κηρύσσετε   (10:7).[1]

Luke's version is similar:

> "And he sent them out to preach . . ."
> καὶ ἀπέστειλεν αὐτοὺς κηρύσσειν (9:2).

We are led to the conclusion that the command, "preach (the
gospel) to all nations," was probably an element in the proto-commission.

Matthew expressly mentions baptism in the commission (28:19).[2]
Luke speaks about "repentance and forgiveness of sins" (24:47), and John
of the disciples' authority to "forgive" and "retain" sins.[3] Since
baptism and forgiveness are related phenomena, it is difficult to know
what was originally contained in the tradition. Perhaps there was some
sort of reference to "baptism (baptize) for the forgiveness of sins."
Such a reference would correspond perfectly with Peter's reply in Acts
2:38 to those who had heard his speech on Pentecost day and wanted to
know what to do: "Repent and be baptized every one of you in the name

---

[1]Cf. Bornkamm, "Der Auferstandene . . .," pp. 181f.

[2]So does Pseudo-Mark: "He who believes and is baptized will be saved"
(16:16a).

[3]Cp. also 1 Cor. 15:1ff. where Paul states that the gospel he preaches
concerns Christ's death for our sins, his resurrection and his appearances to Cephas, the twelve and others.

of Jesus Christ (ἐπὶ τῷ ὀνόματι 'Ιησοῦ Χριστοῦ) <u>for the
forgiveness of your sins</u> (εἰς ἄφεσιν τῶν ἁμαρτιῶν ὑμῶν);[1]
and <u>you shall receive</u> the gift of the <u>Holy Spirit</u>."[2] The author of Acts
may have drawn the sequence of (1) conversion (2) baptism in Jesus' name
(3) resulting in forgiveness of sins and (4) the reception of the Spirit
from Hellenistic Christian missionary preaching. However, there is a
more primitive tradition suggesting the same sequence -- without, of
course, baptism in <u>Jesus'</u> name -- viz., the baptist tradition in Mk. 1:4,
8 (cp. Mt. 3:7-10, Lk. 3:7-9 [Q]).[3] Furthermore, baptism seems to
have been practised in the earliest Palestinian Church as a rite of
initiation in which repentance of sins was central.[4] All of this argues
for the inclusion of a reference to the forgiveness of sins (perhaps
joined to an explicit mention of baptism) in the proto-commissioning.

Although God "the Father" is mentioned by name in Mt. 28:19,
Lk. 24:49 and Jn. 20:22, we cannot be sure that this goes back to the
proto-commission for the following reasons:

> 1. A special emphasis in Johannine theology is that
> the Father's sending of the Son serves both as the
> model and the ground for the Son's sending of the
> disciples.[5]

---

[1] Cp. Lk. 24:47, Jn. 20:23.

[2] Cp. Lk. 24:49, Jn. 20:22, Acts. 10:43-8.

[3] Fitzmyer and R. Dillon, "Acts of the Apostles," <u>JBC</u>, II, p. 175.

[4] Bultmann, <u>Theology of the New Testament</u>, I (ET: Cambridge, 1955),
p. 39; Fuller, p. 85.

[5] Brown, <u>John</u> 29A, p. 1036. See Jn. 13:20, 17:17-19.

2. Luke stresses the fact that the Son can pour out
the Spirit ("the promise of my Father," 24:49)
only because he has received the Spirit from the
Father for this purpose (Acts. 2:33).[1] In other
words, the expression, "the promise of my Father,"
is Luke's way of stressing the fact that Jesus'
role in redemptive history is a gift of God the
Father to him.

3. In Matthew, the reference to the Father is part of
the liturgical formula of baptism in the threefold
name which represents a development from the more
primitive baptism in the name of Jesus alone.[2]

The Holy Spirit is also referred to in all three commissionings
(Mt. 28:19, Lk. 24:49, Jn. 20:22). We are inclined to think that the
proto-commissioning did contain a reference to the future bestowal of
the Spirit.[3] This bestowal would bring about the abiding divine presence
which would make the disciples' missionary endeavors successful. In
Luke, the Spirit is promised at the time of the commissioning (24:49) and
received at Pentecost (Acts 2:1ff.). In John the commissioning and endowment with the Spirit are simultaneous (20:21f.). In Matthew Jesus reassures the disciples that he will remain always with them, and the Holy
Spirit is mentioned only in the baptismal formula. Like the reference
to the Father and Son in the formula, it represents the theological development which led from baptism in Jesus' name only to baptism in the threefold name. It may also have been the case that Matthew felt free to drop
a reference to the bestowal of the Spirit in the commissioning tradition

---

[1] Conzelmann, Luke, p. 174.

[2] See Acts 2:38, 8:16, 10:48.

[3] So Brown, John 29A, p. 1030; Bultmann, John, p. 692, n. 7; cf. Dodd,
Tradition, p. 144, n. 1. All three scholars argue this way from the
actual references to the Spirit in each pericope, but do not elaborate
further.

known to him because of the mention of the Spirit in the baptismal
formula. Furthermore, Matthew prefers to emphasize the idea of the
enduring presence of Jesus (1:23, 18:20, 28:20) rather than that of
the Holy Spirit.[1] We conclude, then, that the proto-commission mentioned a Spirit bestowal.

D. The Reassurance

In the proto-commission the Spirit bestowal just discussed
serves to reassure the disciples: they will be aided in their mission
by the indwelling Spirit.[2] In the subsequent development of the tradition, only Luke keeps the Spirit bestowal as an explicit aspect of the
REASS (24:49). John makes it the prelude to the command to forgive and
retain sins (20:22f.). Matthew, as we just saw, mentions the Spirit
only in connection with the formula of baptism. He alone, under the
influence of the HB commissioning accounts,[3] employs the "I-am-with-
you" formula to convey Jesus' REASS to the disciples.

---

[1]In a pericope discussing the disciples' fate (10:17-25), Matthew draws
from Mark (13:11) the idea that the Spirit will tell them what to say
when arrested (10:19f.), Beare, p. 83. However, Matthew makes one
change in wording here which might shed light on Mt. 28:19 (the baptismal command). He edits Mark's "the Holy Spirit" (13:11) to read, "the
Spirit of your Father" (Mt. 10:20). The wording indicates the close
connection between the Father, the Spirit and Jesus' disciples (Grundmann, Matthäus, p. 293). Since it is spoken by Jesus, it could have
affinities with the triadic baptismal command. See also Mt. 3:16f.
(Jesus' baptism) in which the Spirit descends on him as a dove and the
Father speaks to him.

[2]Cp. Mk. 13:11 pars.; Jn. 14:16f., 26; 15:26; 16:7, 13.

[3]See above, p. 94.

Both Matthew (28:20) and Luke (24:49) employ "and behold,
I . . ." followed by an expression of reassurance.[1] So it is possible
that "and behold . . ." was in the proto-commission. However, caution
is necessary on this point because Luke, like Matthew, employs "behold"
(ἰδού) frequently in his Gospel.[2]

E.   The Conclusion

Only Luke has anything resembling the CONC of HB commissionings: after narrating Jesus' Ascension (24:50f.), he states that the
disciples returned to Jerusalem and blessed God continually in the
temple. Yet the actual carrying out of the missionary command had to
wait until Pentecost. We think, therefore, that it is impossible to
tell if there was a CONC in the proto-commissioning.

F.   Summary

We tentatively suggest that the shape of the original commissioning narrative was as follows:

> CONF   Jesus appeared to the eleven.
>
> REAC   When they saw him they were
>   glad, though some disbelieved.
>
> COMM   Then he said:
>   preach (the gospel)
>   to all nations
>   (Baptize) in my name
>   for the forgiveness of sins.

---

[1] See above, p. 105.

[2] E.g., 1:20, 31, 36, 38, 44, 48; 2:10, 34; 9:39; 10:3 (= "behold, I"),
19 (= "behold, I"); 17:21, 24:4.

REASS   (And behold,) I will send the
Holy Spirit upon you.

V. The *Sitz im Leben* of the Narrative

In Chapter Two[1] we discussed Habel's view that HB call stories
originated in the practice reflected in Gen. 24:34-38 according to which
ambassadors (in this case, Abraham's servant) on a special mission presented their credentials in a specific fashion. We did raise some objections to Habel's stress on the antiquity of the material. Yet his basic
insight about the need for Israel's prophets (viz., Moses, Gideon, Isaiah,
Jeremiah, Ezekiel and Deutero-Isaiah) to present their credentials by
narrating their divine commissioning is accurate. In the same way, anyone among the disciples may have wished to present his credentials for
preaching the dawn of the Messianic age. He would have appealed not only
to the fact of the resurrection but to his having encountered Jesus and
having received a commission to preach the gospel.[2]

---

[1] Pp. 27-9.

[2] All of this is analogous to Habel's statement (323): "If the *Gattung*
arises from the practice of an ambassador publicly presenting his credentials before the appropriate audience, then it seems logical that the
goal of the prophetic formulation of the call in this *Gattung* is to announce publicly that Yahweh commissioned the prophet in question as his
representative." Brown, *John* 29A, p. 973, speaks similarly: "The idea
that the sight of the risen Jesus is an essential part of what consti-
tutes a man an apostle is very similar to the OT idea that a vision of
the heavenly court constituted a man a prophet, enabling him to speak
God's word: Is. 6:1-13, Jer. 1:4ff., 1 Kg. 22:19-22, Ezek. 1-2."
We wish to emphasize that we have here a case of the influence of the
HB commissionings not upon Matthew but upon one of the original disciples.

This opinion is verified by a survey of the manner in which Paul in his letters, and Peter in Acts, appeal to their having seen the risen Jesus. In 1 Cor. 9:1 Paul defends his right to be called an apostle by asking, ". . . have I not seen Jesus our Lord?" Later in the same letter, he seeks to defend the truth of the resurrection against those at Corinth who denied it. He appeals to his having "preached" (εὐηγγελισάμην) to them as of first importance what he himself received, viz., Christ's death for sins,[1] burial and resurrection (15:3f.). He then recounts those to whom Jesus "appeared": Peter (Cephas), the twelve, the more than five hundred brethren, James, all the apostles and, finally, Paul himself (15:5-8). Though he is "the least of the apostles" (15:9), he is still an apostle and a witness to the resurrection. As he tells us in Gal. 1:15ff., Paul's apostolate came through a revelation from God of his Son "in order that I might preach (εὐαγγελίζωμαι) him among the Gentiles (ἔθνεσιν) . . ." (Gal. 1:16).[2] Thus Paul tells us that he has been called to preach the gospel to the Gentile world through an encounter with the risen Jesus. Paul's chief credential for being an apostle to the nations is not his contact with the other apostles at Jerusalem but the fact that Jesus appeared to him (Gal. 1:16f.).[3]

---

[1] The emphasis on dying for sins is consistent with the stress on forgiveness of sins in the proto-commissioning.

[2] Cp. Acts 9:15, 22:21, 26:16-18.

[3] Fitzmyer, "Galatians," JBC, II, p. 239. Cp. the stress on Paul's encounter with the risen Jesus in the Lukan versions of Paul's call: Acts 9:3-6, 22:6-8, 26:13-18.

Turning to the material on Peter, we must exercise more caution since Peter's witness is filtered through Luke's glasses. Peter's
speeches in Acts consistently present the essential facts of the Jesus-
kerygma climaxing in the resurrection and stressing the point that Peter
and the other disciples are witnesses[1] to all that has happened (e.g.,
Acts 2:22-36). This is followed by a call to penance and conversion in
light of the kerygma (e.g., Acts 2:38f.).[2] In some cases, moreover,
there is an explicit reference to baptism (Acts 2:41, 10:47f.). These
same elements (resurrection, witnessing, penance and conversion, baptism)
occur in Peter's other speeches: 3:12-26, 5:29-32, 10:34-48.[3] Although
Lucan theology has shaped these speeches, they are based on "a solid
tissue of pre-Lucan tradition."[4] The term μάρτυς (witness) is typically Lucan. Yet the idea present in each of these speeches that Peter
and the other disciples are witnesses to the resurrection is consistent
with the way in which, in our view, the commissioning tradition came
into existence: as the credentials for preaching of eye-witnesses.[5]

In addition to Peter's speeches in Acts, three other NT
documents mention appearances by the risen Jesus to Peter:

---

[1]Cp. Lk. 24:48; Acts 1:8, 22; 3:15; 5:32; 10:39, 41.

[2]Fitzmyer and Dillon, "Acts," JBC, II, p. 172.

[3]Notice the similarity of the elements to the contents of the proto-
commission.

[4]Fitzmyer and Dillon, "Acts," JBC, II, p. 173.

[5]Cp. the use of "witness" by Paul in his speeches in Acts: 13:31,
22:15, 26:16.

1. ". . . that he <u>was raised</u> (ἐγήγερται) on the third day . . . and that he <u>appeared</u> (ὤφθη) to Cephas . . ." (1 Cor. 15:5).

2. "The Lord has <u>risen</u> (ἠγέρθη) indeed, and has appeared (ὤφθη) to Simon!" (Lk. 24:34).

3. Peter's commission by Jesus at the Sea of Galilee (Jn. 21:15-19).

For several reasons it seems likely that the same event is being referred to in each case. The reports in Luke and 1 Cor. 15 are similar (raised . . . appeared to Simon). The appearance and commissioning by the Sea looks like the first appearance to Peter because 21:3 narrates that Peter had gone back to his occupation as a fisherman as if unaware of a higher calling. Also, Peter's initial failure to recognize Jesus (21:4-7) implies that he had not seen him before. Finally, the rehabilitation of Peter in 21:15-17 (triple profession of love to make amends for the triple denial) is more intelligible if this is Jesus' first appearance to him.[1] The originator of this report of an appearance to Peter and, -- in Jn. 21 -- of a commission, is the apostle himself, and he would have appealed to it as the credential for his own preaching. All of this further emphasizes the need felt by the earliest disciples to ground their apostolic work in an appearance by and commission from the risen Jesus.

In light of the material relating to Peter's commission, it seems that someone other than he -- yet making a similar appeal to an encounter with the risen One -- is responsible for the origin of the tradition about a commissioning of the eleven disciples. The original

---

[1]Brown, <u>John</u> 29A, pp. 1085-87; cf. Fuller, p. 153.

narration of this appearance to the disciples would, therefore, have
been in the first person: "Jesus appeared to us," etc. Its contents
would have been substantially the same as in the proto-commission with
on exception: in light of the controversies about the Gentile mission
in the earliest Church (Acts 15, Gal. 2) we would question the originality of the stress placed upon it. In a more general way, the risen
Jesus commissioned the disciples to spread the gospel. The implications
of this as reflected in such texts as Mt. 28:19, Lk. 24:47, Acts 1:8
("you shall be my witnesses . . . to the end of the earth") were not
immediately evident. Yet within less than 15 years from the time of
Jesus' death and resurrection, as we have shown earlier,[1] the Cornelius
episode (Acts 10) had made clear God's will regarding the Gentile mission.[2]

  Thus, the proto-commissioning, as we have reconstructed it,
took shape within the first 15-20 years after the resurrection at the
hands of someone involved in the Gentile mission who had come in contact
with the tradition about an appearance to and commissioning of the
eleven. Therefore, the proto-commissioning is at least one step removed
from the actual description of Jesus' commissioning which was narrated
by one of the eleven. We have, therefore, two situations in the life
of the early Church which gave rise to the proto-commissioning:

---

[1] Pp. 112-14.

[2] Fitzmyer and Dillon, "Acts," JBC, II, pp. 187f. note that the emphatic
repetition of the vision to Peter (Acts 10:9-16, 11:5-10) and to Cornelius (10:3-8, 30-33) serves to stress the divine direction behind the
Gentile mission.

1. One of the eleven disciples narrated Jesus'
   appearance to them and subsequent commissioning
   so as to authenticate his right to preach the
   gospel of Jesus Christ.[1]

2. A Gentile missionary, at least one step removed
   from the disciple, heard the account of Jesus'
   appearance and commissioning and added the
   universalistic emphasis.

VI. The Matthean Redaction of the Proto-commissioning

Before drawing together the material from Chapters Three and
Four regarding Matthew's redaction of the proto-commissioning, two final
problems must be dealt with: the first involves the derivation of the
declaration of authority (28:18b) and the promise of divine presence
(28:20b); the second involves the triadic baptismal formula (28:19b).

A. The Derivation of Jesus' Words (28:18-20)

Several scholars[2] have correctly noted that the words of the
risen Jesus in Mt. 28:18-20 consist of three elements: the declaration
of authority (18b), the missionary charge (19-20a), the promise of the
abiding presence of Jesus (20b). The same group of scholars draw two
further conclusions about this material: (1) Matthew found each element
separately in the tradition, and (2) redacted them so that they bear
the stamp of his composition. Although the second conclusion is consistent with our analysis of the material in Chapter Three, the first one

---

[1]Besides providing the disciple with credentials for _preaching_ the gospel, the narration of Jesus' appearance was, of course, intended to
authenticate Jesus and his gospel themselves.

[2]Barth, TIM, p. 133, n. 2; Bornkamm, "Der Auferstandene . . .," p. 173;
Fuller, p. 82; Michel, "Der Abschluss . . .," p. 20.

(dealing with the origin of the separate elements) has to be qualified. Certainly, as our preceding discussion in this Chapter has attempted to show, the tradition of a missionary charge was known by Matthew (as it was by Luke and John). On the other hand, the declaration of authority seems to be a Matthean creation influenced directly by Dan. 7:14 as well as indirectly via the Q saying in Mt. 11:27.[1] It corresponds, furthermore, to the divine self-asseveration found in several HB commissionings.[2]

The promise of Jesus' enduring presence also does not appear to be an element which Matthew found in the tradition. Like 1:23 (the "Immanuel" passage), it is a Matthean redactional element.[3] Moreover, it reflects a dominant element in HB commissionings and in the HB generally: that of God's presence with his people.[4]

In contending that the declaration of authority and the promise of divine presence are the work of Matthew himself rather than the pre-Matthean tradition, we are not denying that the theme of the Christ's reception of authority from the Father and that of enduring divine presence were not known before Matthew's time. The former theme is reflected

---

[1]See above, pp. 77-80.

[2]See above, p. 68.

[3]See above, p. 94.

[4]See above, pp. 63-5.

in Mt. 11:27 (Q), the latter in passages which speak of "the Lord's" (or
the Spirit's) assisting presence.[1]

   B. The Derivation of the Triadic Baptismal Formula (28:19b)

          In Chapter One[2] we noted that both Bultmann and Strecker view
the baptismal command as the factor which shaped the composition of Mt.
28:18-20. Although we disagreed with them, we do concur with Strecker's
opinion that Matthew did not himself introduce the triadic baptismal
formula into the practice of his community. There is no other triadic
formula in his Gospel. We also doubt that Matthew would have introduced
a triadic baptismal formula into his Gospel if it were not already the
custom in his community. As we have seen, the earliest practice was that
of baptism into the name of Jesus. In 28:19 we have a practice which
reflects the shift from the Jesus formula of baptism to the triadic one.
That Matthew would put into the mouth of Jesus a triadic baptismal formula without the sanction of the liturgical usage of his church is hard
to believe.[3] Since the commissioning tradition available to Matthew
referred to the forgiveness of sins (and possibly even baptism) in Jesus'
name, and to the promise of the Spirit's assistance, the incorporation
by Matthew of the triadic baptismal formula into the missionary charge
is understandable: "baptizing them in the name of the Father . . . Son
. . . Spirit" (28:19).

---

[1]E.g., Mk. 13:11; Lk. 1:28, 35; 24:49; Acts 1:4f.; 18:10; Jn. 14:16,
26; 15:26; 16:7, 13.

[2]Pp. 4-6.

[3]Strecker, Weg, p. 209.

C. The Matthean Redaction of the Proto-Commissioning

We are now in a position to match our conclusions from Chapter Three against what we have learned about the shape of the proto-commission so as to obtain the clearest picture of Matthew's redactional work. It will be helpful to place side by side the proto-commissioning and the Matthean redaction of it.

Proto-commissioning	Mt. 28:16-20
Jesus appeared to the eleven	Now the eleven disciples went to the mountain in Galilee to which Jesus had directed them.
When they saw him they were glad, though some disbelieved.	When they saw him they worshiped him, though some doubted.
Then he said:	Then Jesus approached and said to them:
	All authority is given to me in heaven and on earth.
preach (the gospel) to all nations (baptize) in my name for the forgiveness of sins.	So go make disciples of all nations, baptizing them in the name of the Father and of the Son and of the Holy Spirit, teaching them to observe all that I have commanded you.
(And behold,) I will send the Holy Spirit upon you.	And behold, I am with you all days till the end of the world.[1]

1. The Mountain in Galilee.

We already concluded[2] that the location of the Christophany on a mountain is the result of Matthean redaction. Only Matthew situates the commissioning, as to its wider venue, in Galilee rather than

---

[1]Translation mine.

[2]P. 71.

Jerusalem (the venue in Luke, John and even Pseudo-Mark). Matthew
thus remains faithful to his Markan source which twice[1] points forward
to an encounter between the disciples and the risen Jesus in Galilee.
This corresponds to the generally greater fidelity of Matthew than of
Luke to the geographical pattern of Mark.[2]

2. Worship and Doubt.

We have already shown[3] that "worship" and "doubt" are characteristic Matthean terms which parallel the comparable terms "be glad"
and "disbelieve" in the proto-commissioning.

3. The Declaration of Authority.

As our preceding discussion has shown, this is a Matthean
redactional element with no parallel in the proto-commissioning.

4. The Missionary Charge.

Πορεύομαι (go) is frequent in Matthew, especially, as we have
seen,[4] in the context of commands or commissionings. Οὖν (therefore) is
redactional[5] and builds a bridge between the declaration of authority

---

[1]Mk. 14:28-Mt. 26:32; Mk. 16:7-Mt. 28:7, 10.

[2]Cf. Conzelmann, Luke, pp. 16, 72f., 93f. Malina (NTS 17), 99, suggests that the Galilean venue helps to tie together the First Gospel's
beginning (Mt. 2:22f.) and its ending (28:7, 10, 16).

[3]Pp. 73-5.

[4]P. 81.

[5]See p. 82.

and the missionary charge. Μαθητεύω (make disciples) is clearly a
Matthean word[1] which replaces the proto-commission's κηρύσσω (preach).
We concluded earlier in this Chapter that πάντα τὰ ἔθνη ("all
nations") was an element in the proto-commission. Its presence there is
one of several reasons which explains the universalistic elements found
not only in 28:19 but elsewhere in the First Gospel.[2]

Based on the conclusions reached earlier in this section, the
triadic baptismal formula appears to be a liturgical element from the
pre-Matthean tradition. Matthew inserted it into the commissioning both
because of its importance for the process of disciple-making[3] and because
it was consistent with three elements in the proto-commissioning:

(1)   baptism (or, at least, forgiveness of sins);

(2)   the mention of the words "in my name" (after "baptize") which run
      parallel to "baptizing them in the name of the Father . . .
      Spirit" (Mt. 28:19);

(3)   the promise of the Spirit's assistance.[4]

The clause, "teaching them to observe all that I have commanded you" is clearly redactional. As we saw earlier[5] each of the
underlined words is used in a distinctive way by Matthew.

---

[1]See p. 82.

[2]See pp. 82-5.

[3]See pp. 86f.

[4]See pp. 117f.

[5]Pp. 88f.

Finally, the promise of Jesus' abiding presence is redactional.[1] It was influenced by the promise of the sending of the Spirit in
the proto-commissioning, as well as by the I-am-with-you expressions in
the HB.

VII. The Results of This Investigation of Mt. 28:16-20

We can now draw together all of our findings and summarize
what has been learned about the concluding verses of the First Gospel.

A. Matthew's Familiarity with the Proto-commissioning

Matthew was familiar with "a primitive apostolic commissioning"
by the risen Jesus. Its _Sitz im Leben_ was one step removed from the
actual narration of a Christophany and commissioning on the lips of one
of the "eleven." It stemmed, rather, from a Gentile missionary who had
come in contact with the narrative of one of the eleven disciples and
added the stress on the Gentile mission ("all nations").

B. The Influence of the Hebrew Bible upon Matthew

Under the influence of the HB generally and of the commissioning tradition particularly, Matthew added certain features which would
give the pericope more clearly the shape of a HB commissioning narrative:
a circumstantial introduction (INT: disciples go to mountain in Galilee);
a statement of authority (28:18b) influenced by Dan. 7:14 and parallel-
ing the "divine self-asseveration" of HB commissionings; the use of "go",
a typical commissioning idiom from the HB; the retention from the

---

[1]See p. 118.

proto-commission of the "nations" theme found in several HB commission-ings;[1] the verb, "command," frequently used in commissionings; the typical expression of reassurance ("I am with you") of HB commissionings; the fourfold use of "all," an adjective frequent in HB commissionings.

C. Mt. 28:16-20 as a Summary of the Whole Gospel

Matthew redacts his material in such a way that he is able to recapitulate several basic themes from the Gospel proper. Since these were already enumerated in the "Conclusions" Section of Chapter Three (p. 96), we will not list them again.

D. The Literary Form of Mt. 28:16-20

Finally, we think we have been able to answer the question which prompted this investigation, that of the literary form or the Gattung of 28:16-20. Wolfgang Trilling was on the right track when he sought for a model in the HB speech-of-God pericopes. After all, most of the commissioning pericopes studied in Chapter Two involved God's speaking a commission (and a word of reassurance) to a patriarch or to a prophet.

C. H. Dodd, though not relating his findings to the HB, came close to isolating the basic shape of the Matthean commissioning and of the other post-resurrection commissionings. We have tried to show that the shape of these commissionings in Matthew, Luke and John was influenced by a primitive apostolic commissioning (the proto-commission). The

---

[1]Specifically, in seven of the twenty-seven pericopes examined.

proto-commission, in turn, was given its shape under the influence of
the HB commissioning form.[1] However, as we just attempted to show in
summary fashion, Matthew has applied the form, as well as the vocabulary,
of HB commissionings more explicitly. This, we feel, is the new element
in the present study which previous investigations have not shown:
Mt. 28:16-20 is a commissioning narrative modeled after those in the HB.
It does not seem surprising that a Gospel so much influenced by the
themes, language and style of the HB should manifest that influence in
its final lines which are the final words of Jesus.

---

[1]Furthermore, as mentioned on p. 120, the account of the Christophanic
commissioning -- as first narrated by one of the eleven disciples --
provided credentials for preaching to the disciple, just as Israel's
prophets used their commissionings as such credentials.

Appendix One THE COMMISSIONING ACCOUNT

IN THE LONGER ENDING OF MARK

(Ps.-Mk. 16:14-20)

I. Introduction

We indicated earlier[1] that we would not base conclusions about
the shape of the proto-commission on Pseudo-Mark because of the difficulty of establishing beyond doubt that it contains material independent
of the other Gospels. Nevertheless, a number of scholars do feel that
independent material is found in Ps.-Mk. 16:14-18.[2] Our own opinion is
that a good case can be made for the independence of Ps.-Mk. 16:15f.,
but probably not of vv. 17f. After a brief comment on the non-Markan
authorship of 16:9-20 and a short analysis of 16:9-13, we shall seek to
justify this viewpoint.

We do not intend to solve the related but distinct problem of
whether or not Mark intended to conclude his Gospel at 16:8.[3] Whatever
the answer given to that question, vv. 9-20 are not the work of the
author of the rest of the Gospel. This is clear for the following

---

[1]Pp. 98f.

[2]See above, p. 98, n. 2.

[3]The case for accepting 16:8 as the intended ending is presented by:
Fuller, pp. 64-68; R. Meye, "The Ending of Mark's Gospel," B Res 14
(1969), 33-43; the case against: Bultmann, HST, pp. 284f.; V. Taylor,
The Gospel according to St. Mark (New York, 1966[2]), pp. 609f.

reasons: (1) The earliest and best textual tradition of Mark terminates at 16:8.[1] (2) The language and style of vv. 9-20 are at variance with the rest of Mark.[2] (3) The verses interrupt the sequence of thought since they do not relate the appearance of the risen Jesus in Galilee, which was promised in 16:7.[3] We therefore concur with the widely accepted view[4] that these verses are an attempt by someone other than Mark to expand upon his extant resurrection narrative (16:1-8).

II. Pseudo-Mark 16:9-13

· The events narrated here pave the way for the final appearance to the eleven and for their commissioning. Two Christophanies are

---

[1]Note especially their absence from Codices Sinaiticus and Vaticanus; and Eusebius' remark that the "accurate" manuscripts end with 16:8 and that 16:9-20 is missing from "almost all manuscripts" (Quaest. ad Marinum 1). See J. K. Elliott, "The Text and Language of the Endings to Mark's Gospel," Theol Z 27 (1971), 255-62; Kümmel, p. 71.

[2]Elliott, 258-61; Taylor, pp. 610-14; H. B. Swete, The Gospel according to St. Mark (New York, 1898), pp. cii-cv.

[3]A. Wickenhauser, New Testament Introduction (ET: New York, 1958), p. 172.

[4]Only one recent study has challenged the view: E. Linnemann, "Der (wiedergefundene) Markusschluss," Z Th K 66 (1969), 255-87. She contends that 16:15-20, though not 9-14, formed part of the original ending of Mark and were preceded by the equivalent of Mt. 28:16-17. Thus, the Markan resurrection narrative consisted originally of Mk. 16:1-8, the equivalent of Mt. 28:16-17 and Mk. 16:15-20. However, she is unable to produce one bit of textual evidence to support this hypothesis. K. Aland responded to her article with his "Der wiedergefundene Markusschluss? (Eine methodologische Bemerkung zur textkritischen Arbeit)" Z Th K 67 (1970), 3-13. He notes, among other methodological errors in her study, Linnemann's theory that Origen took Codices Vaticanus and Sinaiticus with him to Caesarea (this would explain Eusebius of Caesarea's unfamiliarity with her reconstructed text; see p. 135, n. 1). The problem is that Origen died a century before either of these Codices was compiled (Aland, 6).

described, one to Mary Magdalene (vv. 9-11), the other to two unnamed
disciples (vv. 12f.). In both cases a report is made to the rest of
the disciples who do not believe it.

A. The Christophany to Mary

The appearance to Magdalene has affinities with Jn. 20:11-18
(which narrates Jesus' appearance to her and her report of this to the
disciples).[1] However, it also resembles Lk. 24:10-11 by reporting the
disbelief[2] of the disciples. Furthermore, both Ps.-Mk. 16:9 and Lk.
8:2 describe Magdalene as one from whom "seven demons" had been cast out
by Jesus.[3] It appears that Pseudo-Mark has been influenced by Lukan
material -- and perhaps Johannine -- in his description of Mary's
Christophany.

B. The Christophany to the Two Disciples

Ps.-Mk. 16:12f., though not mentioning "Emmaus," resembles Lk.
24:13-35 in the following ways:
(1) It describes a Christophany to "two of them" (δυσὶν ἐξ αὐτῶν,
    16:12=Lk. 24:13).

---

[1]Cp., in particular, "Mary Magdalene went and said to the disciples
(ἔρχεται Μαριὰμ ἡ Μαγδαληνὴ ἀγγέλουσα τοῖς μαθηταῖς)"
(Jn. 20:18) with, "She went and told those (πορευθεῖσα ἀπήγγειλεν
τοῖς) who had been with him" (Ps.-Mk. 16:10). Dodd, "The
Appearances . . .," p. 32.

[2]Both Lk. 24:11 and Ps.-Mk. 16:11 use a form of the verb ἀπιστέω.

[3]Grundmann, Das Evangelium nach Markus (Berlin, 1962), pp. 326f.

140

(2) It describes the two as "walking" or "going" (πορευομένοις,
    16:12=Lk. 24:13) into the "country" (Luke: "village").

(3) It describes how the two "went back and told the rest, but they did
    not believe them" (16:13). Lk. 24:35 reports that the two disciples
    "told what had happened on the road" to the other disciples. The
    disciples' disbelief is not mentioned at this point in Luke, pro-
    bably because Jesus appeared just as the two were reporting their
    Christophany (24:36). However, the disciples' disbelief is mentioned
    subsequently (vv. 38 and 41) in connection with Jesus' appearance to
    them.[1]

We are led to conclude that both Christophanies in Ps.-Mk.
16:9-13 reflect the influence of Luke, and that the first (to Magdalene)
might reflect Johannine influence.

III. Pseudo-Mark 16:14-20

A. Introduction

In Chapter Four[2] we presented a schematization of the commissioning accounts in all four Gospels. The reader is referred back to
it. Except for the absence of a REAC, the Pseudo-Marcan account

---

[1]Taylor, p. 611. See also 24:25 where the Emmaus disciples are chas-
tised by Jesus for being "foolish men, and slow of heart to believe
(πιστεύειν) all that the prophets have spoken!" Note also the
resemblance of this verse to Ps.-Mk. 16:14 where Jesus upbraids the
eleven for their unbelief and hardness of heart.

[2]Pp. 100f.

corresponds to the HB commissioning <u>Gattung</u>. We also listed in Chapter Four[1] the resemblances in the commissionings of Matthew, Luke and John. We now will do the same with Pseudo-Mark.

B. Verbal and Thematic Parallels between

Pseudo-Mark and the Other Gospels

Pseudo-Mark shows the following affinities:

1. With Matthew-Luke-John: continual divine presence (". . . the Lord <u>worked with them</u> (συνεργοῦντος) and confirmed their message by the signs that attended it.").

2. With Matthew and Luke: the universal mission ("Go into all the world and preach the gospel to the whole creation"); mention of the "eleven" disciples (16:14); the authoritative character of Jesus' name ("in my name they will cast out demons . . .," 16:17); the theme of disbelief (16:11, 13, 14, 16).

3. With Matthew: Use of the identical participle, πορευθέντες ("go"), in the missionary charge; express mention of baptism ("He who believes and is baptized will be saved . . .," 16:16).

4. With Luke: the command to preach (κηρύσσω, 16:15); the Ascension (16:19); a CONC stating what the disciples did after the Ascension (16:20).

5. With Luke and John: the Jerusalem venue.[2]

---

[1]Pp. 99, 102-4.

[2]The location of the Pseudo-Marcan commissioning in Jerusalem is inferred from vv. 9-13 which make it clear that all of the appearances occur in the vicinity of that city.

C. Does Pseudo-Mark 16:14-18(20) Contain

Independent Material?

In light of the comparisons drawn in "B" above, we will try to
determine what, if anything, in Pseudo-Mark reflects a version of the
commissioning independent of material drawn from the other Gospels. The
Gattung elements will again provide a logical way to divide the material.
INT: (16:14). "Afterward . . . as they sat at table." ὕστερον is
the last in a series of adverbial expressions: "first" (v. 9), "after
this" (v. 12), "afterward" (or "lastly," v. 14). They tie together the
appearances to Mary, to the two disciples and to the eleven. Though no
other commissioning account explicitly mentions the fact of the disciple's
sitting at a meal, Lk. 24:41-3 narrates Jesus' eating of a piece of
broiled fish as proof that it is he and not a spirit. The availability
of cooked fish presupposes a meal. Furthermore, Lk. 24:30 describes
Jesus as being at table with the two Emmaus disciples.[1]
CONF: (14). ". . . he appeared to the eleven themselves." The identical
verb form, ἐφανερώθη, is used to describe the Christophany to the
two disciples in Ps.-Mk. 16:12. The only other occurrences of φανερέω
in NT resurrection accounts are in Jn. 21. V. 14 has ἐφανερώθη
(just as in Ps.-Mk. 16:12 and 14), and v. 1 ἐφανέρωσεν (twice).
COMM: (14b-16). We already mentioned[2] that Jesus' description of the
Emmaus disciples as "foolish men and slow of heart to believe" (Lk. 24:25)

---

[1]Also, Jn. 21:9-14 describes how the risen Jesus cooked breakfast for
seven of the disciples.

[2]P. 137, n. 1.

resembles Ps.-Mk. 16:14b where the eleven disciples are upbraided for
"their unbelief and hardness of heart."[1] The Pseudo-Markan language is
stronger than the Lukan, and includes the only example of ὀνειδίζω
used of Jesus rebuking his disciples.[2] It reinforces the theme of disbelief and belief which ties Pseudo-Mark's whole account together (16:11,
13, 14, 16, 17).[3] The censure of the disciples might be considered the
negative side of the COMM: It is necessary in view of the disciples'
unbelief.

The COMM proper begins with the participle, πορευθέντες
("go"), exactly as in Mt. 28:19a. The Matthean commissioning may have
influenced Pseudo-Mark here, although he uses the same verb two other
times.[4] Though the remainder of Ps.-Mk. 16:15 contains a universal
missionary charge -- as in Mt. 28:19a -- the wording is distinctive:

> "Go into all the world and preach (κηρύξατε)
> the gospel to the whole creation" (Ps.-Mk. 16:15).

> "Go therefore and make disciples of all nations . . ."
> (Mt. 28:19a).

---

[1] Cp. also to Ps.-Mk. 16:14b, Lk. 24:38 where Jesus asks the eleven,
"Why are you troubled and why do questionings rise in your heart?" A
mild censure may be contained in the question.

[2] Elliott, 259.

[3] The theme has its counterpart in the Markan Gospel proper where the
disciples are described as lacking in understanding of Jesus' person
and mission, e.g., 6:52; 8:17f., 32f.; 9:32. Grundmann, _Markus_, p. 327.

[4] Ps.-Mk. 16:10, πορευθεῖσα; and 16:12, πορευομένοις.

144

If Pseudo-Mark is dependent upon Matthew at this point, it is somewhat
surprising that he does not employ "all nations,"[1] rather than "all the
world" and "the whole creation." Two other NT passages do resemble the
language of Ps.-Mk. 16:15:

> Mk. 14:9   ". . . wherever the gospel is <u>preached in</u>
> the whole world (εἰς ὅλον τόν κόσμον)"
> (Cp. Pseudo-Mark's εἰς τὸν κόσμον ἅπαντα).

> Col. 1:23   ". . . not shifting from the hope of the
> gospel which has been <u>preached to every</u>
> <u>creature</u> (ἐν πάσῃ κτίσει) . . ."
> (Cp. Pseudo-Mark's πάσῃ τῇ κτίσει).

Though Pseudo-Mark obviously knew the Gospel of Mark, his familiarity
with and use of one isolated verse from a Pauline (or deutero-Pauline)
letter seems questionable. And the Markan verse (14:9) does not dupli-
cate Pseudo-Mark's unique combination of "into all the world" and "to
the whole creation."

        We consider it probable, therefore, that Pseudo-Mark drew
upon an independent version of the commissioning tradition in composing
16:15. It resembles the proto-commission and may ultimately have been
derived therefrom.

        The COMM goes on to speak of baptism, but in a manner differ-
ent from Mt. 28:19b where the liturgical and ecclesial aspects are para-
mount. Here, the characteristically Pseudo-Markan theme of belief-
unbelief stands out:

> "He who believes and is baptized will be saved;
> but he who does not believe will be condemned" (Ps.-Mk. 16:16).

---

[1]Lk. 24:47 also has "all nations," and Pseudo-Mark seems quite clearly
to have known Luke. Our discussion of Ps.-Mk. 16:17-20 should make
this even more evident.

The saved-condemned antithesis may have affinities with the Johannine
commissioning:

> "If you forgive the sins of any, they are forgiven;
> if you retain the sins of any, they are retained"
> (Jn. 20:23).[1]

Pseudo-Mark may simply have redacted v. 16 either from Mt. 28:19b or
Jn. 20:23 to fit his belief-unbelief theme. Yet Ps.-Mk. 16:16 is substantially different from either the verse in Matthew or that in John.
So we think that, in composing v. 16, Pseudo-Mark may have had access
to an independent tradition, just as he did in composing v. 15.
REASS: (17-18). The importance of belief is once more stressed:
"those who believe" will receive the ability to perform miraculous deeds
("signs") in conjunction with their missionary work. The Acts of the
Apostles uses the same word, σημεῖα, to describe healings and other
wonderful works performed by the first apostles.[2] Pseudo-Mark, who
knew Luke's Gospel, appears to have drawn his conception of a sign from
Luke's companion volume, Acts.

Furthermore the five signs described can, with one exception
(drinking poison unharmed), be traced to Luke-Acts and Mark, as we
shall now attempt to show.

(1) Exorcism: Mk. 9:38 narrates the report of John of Zebedee to
   Jesus: "Teacher, we saw a man casting out demons (ἐκβάλλοντα
   δαιμόνια, as in Ps.-Mk. 16:17) in your name" (ἐν τῷ ὀνόματί σου,

---

[1]Cp. also Jn. 3:18 to Ps.-Mk. 16:16.

[2]Acts 2:43; 4:16, 22, 30; 5:12; 6:8; 8:13; 14:3; 15:12.

as in 16:17). Lk. 10:17 (the return of the seventy disciples) is similar: "Lord, even the demons are subject to us in your name (ἐν τῳ ὀνόματί σου)."[1]

(2) Glossolalia: the gift of tongues is reported in Acts (2:4, 11; 10:46; 19:6).

(3) Picking up Serpents: This sign again resembles Lk. 10:17-20 (return of the seventy) where Jesus declares that he has given them "authority to tread upon serpents (ὄφεων, as in Ps.-Mk. 16:18) and scorpions . . . and nothing shall hurt you." Pseudo-Mark mentions the fourth sign (drinking poison) and then Jesus' promise that "it will not hurt them."[2]

(4) Drinking Poison Unharmed: This is the only NT mention of such a phenomenon. However, Papias relates that -- among a group of amazing anecdotes which he collected between A.D. 130-40 -- one concerned Justus Barsabbas[3] who did not die though he drank poison.[4] "Here without doubt is the atmosphere of A.D. 100-40."[5] In other words, this sign seems to reflect a relatively late tradition.

---

[1]Cp. also Mk. 10:8: "cast out demons."

[2]Although Luke uses ἀδικέω for "hurt" and Pseudo-Mark βλάπτω, the thought is the same. See also Acts 28:3-6 where Paul is not harmed by a viper.

[3]He is mentioned in Acts 1:23.

[4]Recorded in Eusebius, Hist. Eccl. 3, 39.

[5]Taylor, p. 613.

(5) Healing by Laying on of Hands: The description of Jesus in Mk. 6:5 resembles the description of this phenomenon: "He <u>laid his hands</u> (ἐπιθεὶς τὰς χεῖρας, Ps.-Mk. 16:18 has χεῖρας ἐπιθήσουσιν) upon a few <u>sick people</u> (ἀρρώστοις, 16:18 has ἐπὶ ἀρρώστους) and healed them."[1] Acts records two instances in which cures are performed by the laying on of hands.[2]

CONC: (19-20). Probably the most important passage, however, in terms of overall influence upon Ps.-Mk. 16:17-20 is Mk. 6:12f., the concluding verses to Jesus' sending out of the twelve (6:7-13):

> 6:12 So they <u>went out and preached</u> (ἐξελθόντες ἐκήρυξαν, exactly as in 16:20) that men should repent. (13) And they <u>cast out</u> many <u>demons</u>, and anointed with oil many that were <u>sick</u> and <u>healed</u> them.

As these verses conclude the missionary charge during Jesus' public ministry, Ps.-Mk. 16:17-20 conclude the post-resurrection commissioning.

Ps.-Mk. 16:19 resembles the Lukan Ascension narrative (24:50-3). In both, the Ascension takes place soon after the apostolic commissioning,[3] in the disciples' presence. Both accounts then describe their response to the series of events culminating in Jesus' Ascension: in

---

[1] There are several other examples of Jesus' performance of cures by the laying on of hands: Mk. 5:23 (par. Mt. 9:18); 7:32; 8:23, 25; Lk. 4:40, 13:13.

[2] 9:17, 28:8. In addition, Acts records cases in which the Holy Spirit is imparted by laying on of hands: 8:17, 13:3f., 19:6.

[3] Taylor, p. 613; Stuhlmueller, "Luke," <u>JBC</u>, II, p. 163. The words, "So then the Lord [Jesus] after he had spoken to them," (Ps.-Mk. 16:19) are the final in a series of temporal expressions binding the pericope together (see 16:9, 12, 14).

Pseudo-Mark they begin preaching immediately (16:20); in Luke they return to Jerusalem to bless God in the temple (24:52f.). (The work of preaching must wait until Pentecost in accordance with Luke's time scheme. Cp. Acts 1:12-14.) Only Pseudo-Mark has quoted 2K 2:11 ("was taken up into heaven").[1] It is joined to words derived from Ps. 110:1 ("sat down at the right hand of God"). Although 2K 2:11 is quoted only one other time in the NT (Rev. 11:12), the idea drawn by the first Christians from Ps. 110:1 that the risen Jesus sat down at the right hand of God is a frequent theme in the primitive Church.[2] Pseudo-Mark may have drawn the combination of the two quotes from a tradition associated with the proclamation of the resurrection.[3] He them combined it with the fact of the Ascension which, as we tried to show, he drew from Luke's Gospel.

We already commented on the similarity of 16:20 to Mk. 6:12. The final verse of the Markan Longer Ending summarizes the work of the first apostles and indicates that the signs promised to them came about as a divine confirmation of their message.

IV. Conclusions

The Longer Ending of Mark is composed of three Christophanies, in the last of which Jesus commissions the eleven and then ascends to

---

[1] "Take up" (ἀναλαμβάνω) is used to describe the Ascension in Acts 1:2, 11, 22.

[2] Acts 7:55f.; Rom. 8:34; Eph. 1:20; Col. 3:1; Heb. 1:3, 8:1, 10:12, 12:2; 1 Pet. 3:22; Rev. 3:21. Taylor, p. 613. See also Mk. 14:62 (pars.) and Acts 2:34.

[3] The other possibility is that Pseudo-Mark himself created the statement on the basis of 2K 2:11 and Ps. 110:1. Swete, p. 407, thinks the combination reflects credal language.

heaven. Its unifying theme is the importance of belief in the resurrection. Much of its information is drawn from Luke-Acts, Mark and,
possibly, John. However, we argued that two verses (15f.) may well
reflect the influence of an independent tradition.[1] If this is the
case, then we have further evidence that the proto-commission spoke of
a universal mission to preach and of baptism.[2]

---

[1] This may also be true, as we saw, of 16:19, ". . . was taken up . . .
right hand of God."

[2] See above, pp. 119f.

Appendix Two THE AUTHENTICITY OF THE TRIADIC BAPTISMAL FORMULA

(Mt. 28:19)

I. Introduction

Mt. 28:19 is the only place in the NT using the expression
". . . in the name of the Father and of the Son and of the Holy Spirit,"
and the only place where Father, Son and Spirit are associated in so
formal a way. Elsewhere in the NT, moreover, baptism is performed
simply in the name of Jesus.[1] These facts, by themselves, would probably not have caused the authenticity of the expression to be so widely
discussed among contemporary NT scholars. However, one patristic author,
Eusebius of Caesarea, (263?-340?) quotes 28:19 sixteen times without the
triadic baptismal formula as follows: "go and make disciples of all
nations in my name." The Eusebian testimony has helped to keep the
discussion open.

Our procedure here will consist of two distinct phases:
(1) a detailed examination of the Eusebian testimony and of related
textual considerations;[2] (2) a form critical analysis of the shorter
reading in light of what we learned about Mt. 28:16-20 and about the
proto-commission in Chapters Three and Four respectively, and in light
of evidence from contemporary scholarship.

---

[1] E.g., Acts 2:38, 8:16, 10:48.

[2] We should note from the outset that there is no NT manuscript evidence
whatever of a variant reading of Mt. 28:19.

II. Eusebius' Testimony

As mentioned above, Eusebius quotes 28:19 sixteen times as follows: "go and make disciples of all nations in my name."[1]

πορευθέντες μαθητεύσατε

πάντα τὰ ἔθνη ἐν τῷ ὀνόματί μου.

On five other occasions, however, he quotes 28:19 in accordance with the received text.[2] Consequently, the question arises as to whether or not Eusebius was familiar with manuscript evidence for the shorter reading.

Over seventy years ago, F. C. Conybeare[3] brought the Eusebian testimony to light, and noted that the shorter reading occurs only before the Council of Nicaea (325) and the longer only afterward.[4] He tentatively concluded that the shorter reading is the original one and that the longer was probably created ca. 130-40 to conform to liturgical usage.[5] The most thorough reply to him and defense of the longer

---

[1]The following are the passages in which this reading (hereafter called the "shorter reading") occurs: Demonstr. Evang. 3,6; 3, 7 (twice); 9, 11; Hist. Eccl. III, 5, 2; In Ps. 59, 9; 65, 5; 67, 34; 76, 20; In Is. 18, 2; 34, 16; In Constantin. 16, 8; Theophan. 4, 16; 5, 17; 5, 46; 5, 49.

[2]This reading (hereafter called the "longer reading") occurs as follows: Epist. ad Caesar. 3; Contra Marcell. I, 1, 9; I, 1,36; De Eccl. Theol. III, 5, 22; Theophan. 4, 8. On seven other occasions, Eusebius quotes 28:19 with neither the baptismal formula nor the words "in my name." These are: Demonstr. Evang. 1, 3; 1, 4; 1, 6; In Ps. 46, 4; 95, 3; 144, 9; Theophan. 3, 4.

[3]"The Eusebian Form of the Text Mt. 28:19," ZNW 2 (1901), 275-88.

[4]Ibid., 282.

[5]Ibid., 281, 288.

reading was that of B. H. Cuneo.[1] He clearly establishes that, in some instances at least, Eusebius quotes the NT inexactly.[2] After an analysis of each Eusebian citation of 28:19, he concludes that "When the baptismal command marred the development of his thought, he omitted it; when it was needed in the context, he adduced it."[3]

We now will turn to the Eusebian testimony itself and seek to determine, if possible, the reasons for his use of the shorter reading. Rather than attempting to study every citation of 28:19, we will look at representative passages.

A. The Shorter Reading

Demonstratio Evangelica 3, 7

After describing the disciples' doubts about their ability to preach the gospel to Persians, Armenians, et al., Eusebius continues:

> But while the disciples of Jesus were most likely either saying thus, or thinking thus, the Master solved their difficulties, by the addition of one phrase, saying they should triumph "in my name." For he did not bid them simply and indefinitely make disciples of all nations, but with the necessary addition of "in my name." And the power of his name being so great, that the apostle says: "God has given him a name which is above every name, that in the name of Jesus every knee should bow, of things in heaven, and things in earth, and

---

[1] The Lord's Command to Baptize (Washington, 1923).

[2] Ibid., pp. 95-110.

[3] Ibid., p. 110.

things under the earth" [Phil. 2:9]. He showed
the virtue of the power in his name concealed
from the crowd when he said to his disciples:
"Go and make disciples of all nations in my name."
He also most accurately forecasts the future when
he says: "For this gospel must first be preached
to all the world, for a witness to all nations"
[Mt. 24:14].[1]

The phrases "in my name" (ἐν τῷ ὀνόματί μου) and "in the name

of Jesus" (ἐν τῷ ὀνόματι 'Ιησοῦ) indicate the importance attached   hed

to Jesus' name in the discussion. It is possible that the centrality of

Jesus' name in the overall argument and in the quote from Phil. 2:9 may

have caused Eusebius to quote Mt. 28:19 with the addition of "in my

name."

Demonstratio Evangelica 3, 7

A little later in the same Chapter, while commenting on the

reasons why the uneducated disciples of Jesus succeeded so amazingly in

spreading the gospel, Eusebius concludes that ". . . they could only have

succeeded in their daring venture, by a power more
divine, and more strong than man's, and by the
cooperation of him who said to them: "Make
disciples of all nations in my name" [Mt. 28:19].
And when he had said this he appended a promise,
that would ensure their courage and readiness to
devote themselves to carrying out his commands.
For he said to them: "And lo! I am with you all
days even unto the end of the world." [Mt. 28:20]
Moreover, he is said to have breathed into them a
Holy Spirit, yea to have given them divine and miraculous power -- first saying: "Receive ye the Holy
Spirit" [Jn. 20:22], and then: "Heal the sick,
cleanse lepers, cast out demons; freely ye have
received, freely give" [Mt. 10:8].[2]

---

[1]Translation by W. J. Ferrar, The Proof of the Gospel, V. I (New York,
1920), p. 157. Italics and scripture references mine.

[2]Translation by Ferrar, I, pp. 159f. This passage is nearly duplicated
in Theophania 5, 46.

As in the previous quotation, Eusebius exhibits a tendency to group together various NT passages relating to the same subject. Here, moreover,
he quotes not only from the Matthean version of Jesus' post-resurrection
commission (Mt. 28:19f.) but also from the Johannine (Jn. 20:22). This
is followed by a quote from Mt. 10:8 (Jesus' sending out of the twelve
during his earthly ministry), a passage which has affinities with Ps.-Mk.
16:17f.[1] The Pseudo-Markan verses are part of his commissioning account,
and mention that the disciples will heal, exorcise, etc. in Jesus' name
(ἐν τῷ ὀνόματί μου). Cuneo,[2] moreover, and J. Lebreton[3] may
be right in seeing the influence here of the other post-resurrection
commissioning (besides John and Pseudo-Mark), Lk. 24:47: ". . . repentance and forgiveness of sins should be preached in his name
(κηρυχθῆναι ἐπὶ τῷ ὀνόματι αὐτοῦ) to all nations."

In Psalmis 59, 9

> Eusebius is discussing how Jesus was first sent to Israel.
>
> He said, "I have not come (οὐκ ἦλθον) except to
> the lost sheep of the house of Israel" [Mt. 15:24]. And
> he exhorted his disciples to preach the gospel (κηρύσσειν τὸ
> εὐαγγέλιον)[4] to them [the Jews] first, saying,
> "Go nowhere among the Gentiles, and enter no town of the
> Samaritans, but go rather to the lost sheep of the house
> of Israel" [Mt. 10:5f.]. Then after these [were evange-
> lized] he commanded his disciples to preach the good news
> (εὐαγγελίζεσθαι) to all nations in his name.[5]

---

[1]Cuneo, p. 92.

[2]Ibid., p. 93.

[3]Histoire du Dogme de la Trinité des Origines à St. Augustin, V. I,
Les Origenes (Paris, 1919), p. 560.

[4]Cp. Ps.-Mk. 16:15: ". . . preach the gospel to the whole creation."

[5]Translation mine. Text in J. P. Migne, PG, Vol. 23, Col. 569c.

Both Conybeare and Lebreton[1] consider the final underlined words to be derived from 28:19. However, "preach the good news" has replaced "make disciples," and the words, "to all nations in his name," come close to Lk. 24:47.[2] The passage indicates both Eusebius' grouping together of NT quotations dealing with the same subject and his inexact quoting of Scripture.[3]

Historia Ecclesiastica III, 5, 2

In his discussion of the Jewish War, Eusebius describes how most Christians left Judea. He continues:

> They went on their way to all the heathen teaching their message in the power (δυνάμει)[4] of Christ for he had said to them, "Go and make disciples of all the heathen (ἔθνη) in my name."[5]

Here, admittedly, there is no grouping of texts. Either Eusebius is quoting Mt. 28:19 freely or does, in fact, have textual support for the shorter reading.

B. The Longer Reading

Contra Marcellum 1, 1

Eusebius mentions Paul's admonition to the Galatians that even if he himself or an angel were to preach a gospel different from that

---

[1]Ibid., p. 557.

[2]See discussion of Lk. 24:47 in connection with previous passage, Demonstr. Evang. 3, 7.

[3]See below, pp.156f., for a complete discussion of the latter point.

[4]Cp. Lk. 24:49: "But stay in the city until you are clothed with power from on high."

[5]Translation by K. Lake in Eusebius, The Ecclesiastical History, V. I (Cambridge, Mass.; 1926), p. 199.

which he first preached, he should be accursed (Gal. 1:8).   Eusebius

then asks:

> What was this Gospel? The same which our Saviour
> is said to have given to his disciples, when he
> said to them: "Going make disciples of all the
> nations, baptising them in the name of the Father
> and of the Son and of the Holy Ghost." For he
> alone has favored us with the grace of knowing
> the Holy Trinity by means of the mystical regenera-
> tion. . . . This holy, blessed and mystic Trinity
> of Father and Son and Holy Ghost unto hope of
> salvation through regeneration in Christ, the Church
> of God has received and guards.[1]

The context calls for the triadic formula because both the Trinity and

mystical regeneration (baptism) are mentioned.[2]

De Ecclesiastica Theologia 3, 5

After discussing the distinction of the Son from the Spirit

as a separate person, and also from the angelic spirits, Eusebius con-

tinues:

> None of these spirits can be compared with the
> Comforting Spirit. Therefore this one alone is
> comprised in the holy and thrice-blessed Trinity,
> as also our Lord in commanding his disciples to
> administer baptism to all the nations who would
> believe in him did not order them to administer
> it in any other way than by baptizing them in the
> name of the Father, and of the Son, and of the
> Holy Ghost.[3]

Again the context calls for the triadic formulation.

---

[1] Translation by Cuneo, p. 82.

[2] Ibid., pp. 82f.

[3] Translation by Cuneo, p. 83.

Theophania 4, 8

The same work (5, 46) also includes a quotation of 28:19 with the shorter reading. In the present passage, Eusebius gives us an almost exact quotation of Mt. 28:16-20[1] which is followed later in the text by:

> But of necessity did he add the mystery of cleansing. For those who should be converted among the heathens, he had to cleanse by his power from all pollution and uncleanness, because they had been defiled by their demoniac and polytheistic error, and had been laden with uncleanness of all sorts, but now had for the first time renounced that life of abomination and lawless practices. These very persons, then, did he admonish to teach after this cleansing through his mystic doctrine . . . the observance of all things which he had commanded them.[2]

The expression "cleansing through his mystic doctrine" is unusual, but would seem to refer to baptism.[3] Support is lent to this view by referring again to the first example of the Longer Reading (Contr. Marc. 1, 1) in which Eusebius, right after mentioning baptism in the name of Father, Son and Spirit, talks of "knowing the Holy Trinity by means of the mystical regeneration."

---

[1] The only significant change is his addition of the words "by my Father" (ὑπὸ τοῦ πατρός μου, cp. Mt. 11:27) after "All authority in heaven and on earth has been given to me." Yet the change again indicates Eusebius' tendency to quote inexactly.

[2] Translation by Cuneo, p. 84. Cp. last clause (after break in text) to Mt. 28:20a.

[3] Cuneo, ibid.

C. Quotations of 28:19 with Neither the Shorter

Nor the Longer Reading

Demonstratio Evangelica 1, 4

Commenting upon the "New Law" brought by Jesus for dissemination throughout the world, he asks:

> Which is the New Law which shall go out of Sion
> other than the Gospel, which through our Savior
> Jesus Christ and through his disciples, was
> disseminated through the world, according to the
> words which he spoke to his disciples: "Going make
> disciples of all the nations, teaching them to
> observe all things whatsoever I have commended you."[1]

The center of focus is the universal missionary command as it relates to teaching the "New Law" brought by Jesus. The mention of baptism might be thought out of place here.

In Isaia 41, 10

> He [Jesus] encouraged this option: that they
> fearlessly preach the gospel to all nations
> (εἰς πάντα τὰ ἔθνη κηρῦξαι τὸ εὐαγγέλιον).
> Indeed, he also revealed himself as Savior
> in the Gospels when he said: "behold, I am
> with you always to the close of the age"
> [Mt. 28:20].[2]

The final sentence is an exact quotation of Mt. 28:20b, and leads one to suppose that "preach the gospel to all nations" derives from 28:19. However, Eusebius' words, more closely resemble Mk. 13:10: "And the Gospel must first be preached (δεῖ κηρυχθῆναι τὸ εὐαγγέλιον) to all nations."[3] Eusebius' habit of quoting the NT inexactly is once again evident.

---

[1] Translation by Cuneo, p. 72.

[2] Translation mine. Text in PG 24, Col. 377d.

[3] Cp. also Lk. 24:47 and Ps.-Mk. 16:15.

D. Other Eusebian Variations from the Received Text of the NT

An examination of other passages in which Eusebius deviates from the received text may shed light on the question of Mt. 28:19. Some of these changes are in the nature of minor paraphrases, the sort of thing which a preacher might do during a sermon. Others involve either the addition or deletion of a phrase or clause, or the combination of two NT passages.

(1) An important case in point is Mt. 11:27:

> All things have been delivered to me by my Father;
> and no one knows the Son except the Father, and
> no one knows the Father except the Son and any one
> to whom the Son chooses to reveal him.

In four of the twelve cases in which all or part of 11:27 is quoted by Eusebius, he inserts after, "no one knows the Son except the Father," these words: "alone who has begotten him (εἰ μὴ μόνος ὁ γέννησας αὐτόν)." The inserted words, which resemble Jn. 1:13, indicate that Eusebius quoted scripture inexactly and felt free to add words to a text drawn from or resembling another text.

(2) Cuneo[1] provides sixteen examples in which Eusebius combines two distinct NT passages. Two examples of this will suffice.

(a) In De Theol. Eccles. 1, 20, Eusebius combines 1 Tim. 6:16 with a paraphrased portion of Jn. 1:9f.:

> and [God] is light inaccessible, as the divine
> Apostle teaches when he says: "inhabiting light
> inaccessible, whom no one has seen, nor is able
> to see [1 Tim. 6:16]. But he was in the world
> enlightening every man coming into the world"
> [Jn. 1:9f. partially].[2]

---

[1]Pp. 107ff.

[2]Translation ibid., p. 107.

Eusebius attributes the entire combined passage to the "divine Apostle" (Paul) despite the use of the Johannine verses.

(b) A similar phenomenon occurs in In Ps. 61, 6-9 where Eusebius attributes to the "divine Apostle" a passage combining Rom. 3:24 and 1 Jn. 2:1f.

E. Summary of the Eusebian Testimony

(1) Eusebius knew and used the received text of Mt. 28:19.

(2) He clearly is capable of quoting the NT inexactly and of combining or at least grouping in close proximity passages which relate in some way to each other. These tendencies of his argue for the conclusion that the shorter reading is not based upon textual evidence, but represents instead a free use of 28:19 combined with "in my name," a phrase widely used in the NT.[1] In particular, it is used in the Lukan post-resurrection commissioning (24:47)[2] and the Pseudo-Marcan (16:17).

(3) Nevertheless, a special prominence is given to the shorter reading and to the related notion of the importance of Jesus' name, especially in one work, the Demonstratio Evangelica.[3] It therefore

---

[1] See below, p. 169.

[2] Luke has ἐπὶ rather than ἐν τῷ ὀνόματι, but the meaning is the same.

[3] One could even conjecture that Eusebius knew a text which added "in my name" before the baptismal formula (= a combination of the shorter and longer reading). He eventually became aware that this combination text was eccentric and dropped "in my name." This proposal must remain conjectural since Eusebius never quotes 28:19 in such a form.

remains possible -- but not, in our opinion, probable[1] -- that Eusebius had textual support for the shorter reading of 28:19.

III. Patristic Data Aside from Eusebius

As noted earlier, there simply is not any other patristic source which would corroborate the originality of the shorter reading. Several scholars[2] have appealed to the Didache to support the longer reading. Did. 7:1, 3 reads as follows:

> Now concerning baptism. Baptize as follows when
> you have rehearsed the aforesaid teaching. Baptize
> in the name of the Father and of the Son and of the
> Holy Spirit (εἰς τὸ ὄνομα τοῦ πατρὸς καὶ τοῦ υἱοῦ
> καὶ τοῦ ἁγίου πνεύματος) in running water. (Did.
> 7:1) . . . But if you have neither,[3] pour water
> on the head three times -- in the name of the Father,
> Son and Holy Spirit (Did. 7:3).[4]

The Greek of "in the name of . . . Holy Spirit" is identical to that in Mt. 28:19. What calls the value of the parallel between 28:19 and Did. 7:1, 3 into question is this: the most probable date of the Didache is the first half of the second century.[5] This would put it rather close to the date which Conybeare conjectures for the interpolation

---

[1]Cp. Lebreton's conclusions, p. 560. E. Schweizer, "Πνεῦμα, Πνευματικός" (TWNT, VI, p. 401, n. 440) thinks that Eusebius' shorter reading "may be an abbreviation of his own."

[2]E.g., Bornkamm, "Der Auferstandene . . .," p. 186, n. 59; Fuller, p. 87; Strecker, Weg, p. 209, n. 6.

[3]That is, neither "running water" nor a pool of some sort.

[4]Translation by R. Kraft in The Apostolic Fathers, III (New York, 1965), pp. 163f.

[5]H. Köster, Synoptische Überlieferung bei den Apostolischen Vätern (Berlin, 1957), p. 159; cp. J. Quasten, Patrology (Westminster, Md.; 1962) V. I, p. 37.

of the baptismal command into Mt. 28:19 (ca. 130-40). If he is correct, both the Didache and the longer (baptismal) reading could have sprung from the liturgical practice of the second century. Both would be later than the shorter and -- if Conybeare is correct -- original reading. The Didache's usefulness in confirming the authenticity of the longer reading is, therefore, questionable.

IV. A New Jewish Christian Source of Mt. 28:19?

S. Pines[1] recently discovered a document which, though ostensibly a Moslem anti-Christian polemic dating from the tenth century, appears to be derived from a Jewish Christian community of perhaps the fifth or sixth century who wrote in Syriac.[2] He provides a translation of the Jewish Christian source and notes one passage which may parallel Mt. 28:19-20:[3]

> He [Jesus] and his companions behaved constantly
> in this manner,[4] until he left this world. He
> said to his companions: "Act as you have seen me
> act, instruct people in accordance with instructions
> I have given you, and be for them what I have been
> for you." His companions behaved constantly in this
> manner and in accordance with this (70a).[5]

---

[1] "The Jewish Christians of the Early Centuries of Christianity according to a New Source," Proceedings of the Israeli Academy of Sciences and Humanities II (Jerusalem, 1968), pp. 237-310.

[2] Pines, pp. 237, 301.

[3] "But the quotation in the text -- if indeed it corresponds to the verses -- has been amplified." Pines, p. 261, n. 92.

[4] "I.e., they observed the commandments of the Mosaic Law." Ibid., p. 261, n. 90.

[5] Text ibid., p. 261.

Pines' colleague, D. Flusser,[1] has taken up and amplified his suggestion
that the passage may have adapted material from Mt. 28:19f. "Act as you
have seen me act" is considered by him an adaptation of Jn. 13:15 intended
to show that, as Jesus observed the commandments of the Law, his followers
also should.[2] The words which follow, "instruct people in accordance
with instructions I have given you, and be for them what I have been for
you," reflect the Eusebian form of 28:19, according to Flusser. The words,
"instruct people . . . given you," parallel "teaching them to observe all
that I have commanded you;"and "be for them . . . for you" paraphrase the
"in my name" of the Eusebian emendation.[3] If "act as you have seen me
act" is considered an adaption of Jn. 13:15, then "be for them what I have
been for you" could be an adaptation of Jn. 20:21 just as well as of Mt.
28:19 (shorter reading). Jn. 20:21 reads: "As the Father has sent me,
even so I send you." We think, therefore, that Flusser is on thin ice
when he tries to use this passage to propound the view that the shorter
reading of Mt. 28:19 is original.

V. The Manuscript Situation

As noted in the "Introduction," there is no manuscript evidence for the shorter reading of 28:19. If it is the original reading,
one is naturally led to ask why not a single manuscript containing it

---

[1]"The Conclusion of Matthew in a New Jewish Christian Source," ASTI
5 (1967), 112ff.

[2]Ibid., 113f.

[3]Ibid., 114.

survived in the Church.[1] Conybeare attempted to answer this type of
objection in a later article[2] by appealing to dogmatic developments
within the Church. Long before the year 400, he claims, the equality
of the Holy Spirit within the Trinity had been decided. Thus the received text of Mt. 28:19 with its mention of baptism in the name of
Father, Son and Spirit would have been so invaluable to the dominant
party that it "could not but make its way into every codex, irrespec-
tively of its textual affinities."[3] Even if the longer reading was made
as early as Conybeare suggests (ca. 130-40), we would question the total
disappearance of the shorter reading. The "dominant party," as Conybeare
terms it, must be credited with great thoroughness in correcting all
extant manuscripts of Matthew.[4]

<h3 style="text-align:center">VI. Form Criticism and Mt. 28:19</h3>

Preliminary Remarks

In reconstructing the proto-commission, we left open the question of whether there was an express mention of baptism. Thus, this part
of the reconstruction reads: "preach (the gospel) to all nations, (baptize)
in my name for the forgiveness of sins. (And behold,) I will send the

---

[1]Lebreton, p. 555.

[2]"Three Early Doctrinal Modifications of the Text of the Gospels,"
Hibbert Journal 1 (1902), 96-113.

[3]Ibid., 108. By the "dominant party" Conybeare is referring to those
in the Church who supported the consubstantiality of the Son and the
Holy Spirit with the Father.

[4]F. J. Chase, "The Lord's Command to Baptize (Mt. 28:19)," Journal of
Theological Studies 6 (1905), 499.

166

Holy Spirit upon you."[1] We then examined the Matthean redaction of the proto-commission, and concluded that Matthew did not himself compose the triadic baptismal formula but drew it from the usage of his church.[2] The shorter reading ("make disciples of all nations in my name") corresponds better in some respects to the proto-commission. One might even argue that it was not Matthew who inserted the triadic baptismal formula but a later scribe. On the other hand, the following arguments stand in opposition to the shorter reading:

(1) The proto-commission may, in fact, mention baptism and does mention forgiveness of sins and the promise of the Holy Spirit (both of which are associated with baptism).

(2) In the actual exegesis of 28:19-20a (the COMM), we concluded that both baptizing and teaching were logical aspects of disciple-making ("go . . . and make disciples"), and corresponded to a theme found elsewhere in the First Gospel: regulation of the community.[3]

In light of these observations based upon conclusions arrived at in Chapters Three and Four, we will now examine and evaluate the form critical findings of several scholars, all of whom cast doubts on the originality of the longer reading.

---

[1] See above, pp. 119f.

[2] See above, p. 127.

[3] See above, pp. 86f.

A. David Flusser

D. Flusser[1] attempts to support the shorter reading by appealing to the rabbinic practice whereby a teaching was handed down by means
of the expression, "Rabbi X says in the name of Rabbi Y."[2] This practice is reflected in NT passages where the apostles are said to have
spoken, preached and taught in the name of Jesus (Acts 4:17f.; 5:28, 40;
9:27-9).[3] In the context of Mt. 28:19f., "teaching them to observe all
that I have commanded you" (v. 20a), is an explanation of "Go make disciples of all nations in my name." Only the shorter reading of 28:19
is really coherent because it keeps together (1) "make disciples of all
nations," and (2) "teaching them to observe all that I have commanded
you." Jesus taught the disciples and they on their part must teach the
nations "in his name."[4]

Although it is an exaggeration to say that only the shorter
reading is coherent, Flusser's argument is quite persuasive. The
strongest objection to it is that within the Christian community baptizing and teaching were interrelated aspects of the apostolic mission.
Several passages in Acts not only indicate this interrelatedness but also
the fact that teaching followed baptism (just as in 28:19-20, received
text).[5]

---

[1]"Conclusion of Matthew . . .," 110-20. Flusser, as noted earlier (p.
160), also appeals both to the Eusebian testimony and to the newly
discovered Jewish Christian document in support of his position.

[2]Ibid., 111. He cites an example from Pirke Aboth 6,6: "He who repeats
a thing in the name of him who said it brings deliverance to the world."

[3]Ibid.

[4]Ibid., 112.

[5]Acts 2:37-42, 8:12f., 9:18f., 10:34-48, 16:13-15, 18:8-11.

B. Ernst Lohmeyer

Influenced by the Eusebian data, E. Lohmeyer argues that both forms of 28:19 existed in the primitive Church.[1] Lohmeyer relates his theory to his more general idea that primitive Christianity had a two-fold origin in Jerusalem and in Galilee. This is reflected in the two versions of 28:18-20 (the longer reading and the shorter). The longer springs from a primitive Galilean Christianity which considered baptism as a necessary condition of salvation and traced the triadic form of baptism back to Jesus' own baptism when the Spirit descended upon him and the Father blessed him ("Thou art my beloved Son . . .," Mk. 1:9-11 and pars.). The shorter springs from the Jerusalem tradition which did not regard the sacrament of baptism, originating from John, but the imitation of Jesus (discipleship) as the key criterion of the eschatological fellowship.[2] Lohmeyer reconstructs the shorter reading so as to form the following poetic pattern.

1. To me is given all authority
    in heaven and on earth,

2. Therefore go, make disciples of all nations
    in my name

3. And teach them to observe all
    that I have commanded you.

4. And behold, I am with you all days
    until the end of the age.[3]

---

[1] "'Mir ist gegeben alle Gewalt!' -Eine Exegese von Mt. 28:16-20," in In Memoriam Ernst Lohmeyer (Stuttgart, 1951), pp. 28ff.

[2] Lohmeyer, p. 32.

[3] Lohmeyer, p. 29; my translation from the German.

Four lines are thus recognizable in each of which a 3-2 stress pattern
is present. This corresponds to a rhythmic poetic pattern which existed
when the commission first took shape in Aramaic.[1] The middle lines (2
and 3) have an analogous construction: a participle followed by a verb.[2]
All four lines employ the adjective "all," each time occurring in the
first half of the line. The baptismal command does not fit into this
poetic structure and is, therefore, a later insertion into the text.
The insertion was made possible because the missionary command existed
in a pre-Matthean Aramaic form which, in Galilee, included the baptismal
command. Matthew himself adopted the Jerusalem version ("in my name"),
but the presence of baptismal command in the Galilean tradition led to
its later being inserted into the Matthean Gospel.[3]

Although questions have been raised about the validity of
Lohmeyer's twofold origin theory,[4] we will -- after summarizing Kosmala's
similar theory -- raise doubts about the positions of both men on form
critical grounds.

---

[1] Lohmeyer, ibid.

[2] Though Lohmeyer does not say so, he is presumably referring to the
Greek (and Aramaic?) version of these lines where the participle-verb
pattern would be present. In German, the participles have been transferred into the imperative mood ("gehet," line 2; "lehrt," line 3).

[3] Ibid., pp. 30, 32ff.

[4] See, e.g., J. Rohde, Rediscovering the Teaching of the Evangelists (ET:
Philadelphia, 1968), p. 90.

C. Hans Kosmala

Also under the influence of the shorter reading in Eusebius,
H. Kosmala[1] considers the baptismal command a later insertion to the
text of 28:19. Like Lohmeyer, he divides 28:18-20 into four lines and
sets them up in Greek as follows:[2]

ἐδόθη μοι πᾶσα ἐξουσία ἐν οὐρανῷ καὶ ἐπὶ γῆς.

πορευθέντες μαθητεύσατε πάντα τὰ ἔθνη ἐν τῷ ὀνόματί μου

διδάσκοντες αὐτοὺς τηρεῖν πάντα ὅσα ἐνετειλάμην ὑμῖν.

καὶ ἰδοὺ ἐγὼ μεθ' ὑμῶν εἰμι πάσας τὰς ἡμέρας ἕως τῆς

     τῆς συντελείας τοῦ αἰῶνος

The poem which results is not, however, a Greek one to be scanned, as in
Greek poetry. Rather it is "most likely a translation from Hebrew;
after all it is meant to be a saying of Jesus."[3] Retranslation into
Hebrew, though, would be futile because we do not know whether the Greek
translation is literal or merely a paraphrase. Still, the progressive
structure of the whole and the interrelationship between the four lines
is discernible. It resembles a well-constructed Hebrew poem:

1. All power is given unto me in heaven and on
   earth.

2. (a) Go and make all nations disciples in my name,
   (b) Teaching them to observe all that I have
        commanded you.

---

[1]"The Conclusion of Matthew," ASTI 4 (1965), 132-47.

[2]Ibid., 138.

[3]Kosmala, 139.

3. And behold, I am with you all the days till
the consummation of the aeon.[1]

Line 1 states that Jesus has risen to universal power. Lines 2a and 2b
express the commissioning of the disciples to make this message known to
the nations. Line 2a refers to the fact of making disciples; 2b to the
means for carrying this out: by teaching the nations to observe Jesus'
commandments. Line 3 reassures the disciples that Jesus will always be
present with them. While lines 2a and 2b exemplify what in Hebrew poetry
is called "synthetic parallelism," lines 1 and 3 are related in a different way: the statement in 3 is dependent upon that in 1. Only by
possessing universal authority can Jesus remain always with his disciples.
So these two lines enclose the missionary charge. Thus the important
conclusion of the First Gospel is expressed "in a suitable poetic form."[2]

In noting the absence of a CONC in Mt. 28:16-20,[3] we stressed
the poetic quality of these final verses. Lohmeyer's and Kosmala's observations tend to corroborate this except that they see the poetic
structure as vitiated if the baptismal command is retained. This, we
feel, is not necessarily the case:

1. All authority is given to me in heaven and
on earth.

---

[1] Translation by Kosmala, ibid.

[2] Kosmala, 139f.

[3] See above, p. 69f.

> 2. So go make disciples of all nations,
>   (a) baptizing them in the name of the Father
>   and of the Son and of the Holy Spirit,
>   (b) teaching them to observe all that I have
>   commanded you.
>
> 3. And behold, I am with you all days till
>   the end of the world.[1]

Here the commissioning falls into the threefold pattern identified by

many scholars.[2] After (1) the statement of authority Jesus gives (2)

the universal missionary charge and specifies that it is to be accom-

plished by baptizing and teaching. Then (3) the word of assurance con-

cludes the commission.

Neither Lohmeyer's Aramaic poetic scheme nor Kosmala's Hebrew

one seems very probable. Lohmeyer is presuming that Matthew found the

Semitic poem in his tradition in a form closely approximating its final

shape. Yet we have tried to show[3] that Matthew has taken a tradition

about a missionary charge to the eleven disciples and shaped it quite

distinctively to his own purposes. Kosmala, though not sure whether the

Greek version of 28:18-20 is a literal translation of the Hebrew original

or only a paraphrase,[4] commits the same error as Lohmeyer (unless we are

to assume that Matthew first composed the charge in Hebrew and then put

it into a comparable Greek form). We would be more convinced of the

---

[1]Translation mine.

[2]E.g., Bornkamm, "Der Auferstandene . . .," p. 173; Strecker, _Weg_, p. 210.

[3]Pp. 125ff.

[4]Kosmala, 137.

validity of the Semitic poetry theories if Matthew were in the habit of writing such poetry elsewhere in his Gospel. The Lord's prayer (6:9ff.) is somewhat poetic, but seems to reflect the influences of liturgical -- rather than formally poetic -- usage.[1]

Kosmala also argues for the originality of the shorter form of 28:19 by appealing to the emphasis on Jesus' name in Matthew. His infancy narrative stresses Jesus' name much more than Luke's (cp. Mt. 1:21-25 with Lk. 1:31 and 2:21). Any who gather in Jesus' name can be sure of his presence with them (Mt. 18:20; no par.). In Mt. 19:29, Mk. 10:29 and Lk. 18:29 Jesus demands that his followers leave everything: "for my name's sake" (Mt.), "for my sake and the gospel's" (Mk.), "for the sake of the kingdom of God" (Lk.). When Jesus first sent out his disciples, he warned them they would be hated "by all for my name's sake" (Mt. 10:22; no par.). Mk. 13:13 and Lk. 21:12, 17 (the Synoptic apocalypse) do mention persecution for the sake of Jesus' name, but the Matthean parallel (24:9) expands Mark's "hated by all" to "hated by all nations (πάντων τῶν εθνῶν)[2] for my name's sake." Just as the disciples will be hated by all nations for the sake of Jesus' name (Mt. 24:9), so they will make all nations disciples in his name (28:19, shorter reading).[3]

---

[1] Cf. Stendahl, PCB, p. 778.

[2] Cp. Mt. 28:19a.

[3] Kosmala, 142.

There can be no doubt that the importance attached to Jesus' name is a Matthean characteristic. The longer reading of 28:19 does not diminish this importance. It might even be thought to enhance Jesus' name by giving it a parallel stature with the name of the Father[1] and of the Holy Spirit (". . . in the name of the Father and of the Son and of the Holy Spirit . . .").

D. Paul Gaechter

One other proposal on the original wording of 28:19 should be mentioned briefly. P. Gaechter[2] suggests that 28:19 read as follows in its "original form:"

> So macht denn alle Völker zu meinem Schülern,
> indem ihr sie tauft in meinem Namen.
>
> So then make all nations my disciples,
> by baptizing them in my name.

Gaechter provides no grounds for this reading nor does he tell us whether it ever existed as such in the written Gospel of Matthew or only orally. The parallel between "zu meinem Schülern" and "in meinem Namen" might provide some justification for this reading. Also, the practice of baptism in Jesus' name in Acts corresponds with this reading.[3] Although Gaechter has provided a reading which is close to the shorter one

---

[1] Cf. Mt. 6:9: "Our Father . . . hallowed be thy name."

[2] Die Literarische Kunst im Matthäus-Evangelium (Stuttgart, 1966), pp. 78f.

[3] E.g., Acts 2:38, 8:16, 10:48. Note also Stendahl's comment: "On the other hand, a reference to the practice of the church [baptism] (with or without a trinitarian formula) is well in keeping with this epiphany, which pictures the situation of the church in all its other details" (PCB, p. 798).

found in Eusebius, it actually corresponds neither to the shorter nor
to the longer reading. Since it also lacks support either in any NT
manuscript or in a patristic source, it must remain very conjectural.

VII. Conclusions

It is not possible to rule out altogether the shorter reading.
Both the Eusebian evidence and the form critical and exegetical findings[1] of Flusser make this the case. Moreover, the presence of "in my
name" in the proto-commission lends some credibility to the shorter
reading.

On the other hand, the lack of manuscript evidence for the
shorter reading and of patristic evidence (aside from Eusebius) are
serious objections to its acceptance. So is the fact that Eusebius was
in the habit of quoting scripture inexactly. Moreover, we raised several
questions about the arguments of those scholars who support the originality of the shorter reading. Finally, our own form critical and exegetical findings tend to support the fact that Matthew incorporated the
baptismal command from the practice of his church into his Gospel. It
is not an unreasonable development, we feel, from, "(baptize) in my name
for the forgiveness of sins. I will send the Holy Spirit upon you;" to,
"baptizing them in the name of the Father . . . Holy Spirit . . . I am
with you always." In short, we think that the triadic baptismal formula
has a strong probability of being authentic.

---

[1]Esp., "Rabbi X says in the name of Rabbi Y."

Appendix Three THE USE OF THE COMMISSIONING <u>GATTUNG</u>

IN MATTHEW 28:1-10

Matthew also employs the commissioning <u>Gattung</u> in the other two epiphanies of his resurrection narrative. The schematization below makes clear the parallel form of the three epiphanies in Ch. 28. In addition, Matthean vocabulary ties the three together: "worship" (vv. 9, 17); "see" (vv. 6, 7, 10, 17); "approach" (vv. 9, 18); "go" (vv. 7, 19); "fear" (vv. 4, 5, 8, 10); "tell" (vv. 8, 10). Also, "(and) behold . . ." runs like a unifying thread through the whole resurrection narrative: vv. 2, 7 (twice), 9, 11, 20.

	28:1-8 (Angelophany)	28:8-10 (Christophany)	28:16-20 (Christophany)
INT	(1) Two Marys went to the tomb.	(8) Women were going from tomb to tell disciples about resurrection (= CONC of 28:1-8).	(16) Disciples went to appointed mountain in Galilee.
CONF	(2-3) Angel appeared and rolled back stone.	(9) Jesus met them and said, "Hail!"	(17a, 18) Jesus came (approached, προσελθών) and spoke to them.
REAC	(4) Guards faint and women are frightened. [1]	(9) They approached, took hold of his feet and worshipped (προσεκύνησαν) [2] him.	(17) Seeing (ἰδόντες) him they worshipped him (προσεκύνησαν), but some doubted.
COMM	(5b-7) Go (πορευθεῖσαι) tell his disciples he is risen and will see (ὄψεσθε) them in Galilee.	(10b) Tell (ἀπαγγείλατε) my brethren to go to Galilee where they will see (ὄψονται) me.	(19-20a) Go (πορευθέντες) and make disciples of all nations . . .

---

[1] The women's fear at the sight of the radiant angel is not expressly mentioned here but is clear from v. 8: "They went away quickly from the tomb with fear (φόβου) and great joy . . ." However v. 8 also makes it evident that their fear was of the nature of reverential awe rather than the paralyzing terror of the guards. Cf. Filson, Matthew, p. 301.

[2] Neirynck, NTS 15, 178f., discusses the parallel use of προσκυνέω in vv. 9 and 17. The women do not take hold of Jesus' feet so as to verify that it is really he, but as part of their gesture of worship. Cp. Acts 10:25 and LXX 4 Kg. (= 2 Kg.) 4:37.

REASS (5a)[1] Do not be afraid (μὴ φοβεῖσθε); for I know that you seek Jesus . . .

(10a) Do not be afraid (μὴ φοβεῖσθε).

(20b) I am with you always . . .

CONC[2] (8) They went away quickly and ran to tell (ἀπαγγεῖλαι) the disciples.

(11a)[3] While they were going . . .

---

[1] In the first two epiphanies the REASS precedes the COMM, but follows it in the final epiphany.

[2] Though 28:16-20 lacks a CONC, Matthew's use of one in the other two epiphanies is proof of his familiarity with this element of the HB commissioning Gattung. See again our explanation for his not using one in 28:16-20, pp. 69f. above.

[3] Although these words are part of the next pericope (the legend about the guards), they serve as a conclusion for the second epiphany by pointing out that the women did as Jesus directed them.

BIBLIOGRAPHY

I. Primary Texts

Biblia Hebraica, R. Kittel (ed.). Stuttgart, 1951.[7]

Didache, R. Kraft (ed.). The Apostolic Fathers, V. III. New York, 1965.

Eusebius, Historia Ecclesiastica, E. Schwartz (ed.). Kirchengeschichte. Berlin, 1952.[5]

_____, The Ecclesiastical History, V. I. K. Lake (trans.). Cambridge, Mass.; 1926.

_____, Opera, J. P. Migne (ed.). Patrologiae cursus completus Series Graeca. Vols. 23-4. Paris, 1875-87.

_____, The Proof of the Gospel, V. I. W. J. Ferrar (trans.). New York, 1920.

Novum Testamentum Graece, E. Nestle (ed.). Stuttgart, 1963.[25]

Pirke Aboth, R. Travers Herford (ed. and trans.). The Ethics of the Talmud: Sayings of the Fathers. New York, 1945.

Septuaginta, id est Vetus Testamentum Graece juxta LXX interpretes, A. Rahlfs (ed.). Stuttgart, 1950.[4]

_____, Vetus Testamentum Graecum auctoritate Societas Litterarum Gottingensis editum. V. 14, Isaias (ed. J. Ziegler, 1967); V. 15, Jeremias, Baruch, Threni, Epistula Jeremiae (ed. Ziegler, 1957); V. 16, pt. 1, Ezechiel (ed. Ziegler, 1952); V. 16, pt. 2, Susanna, Daniel, Bel et Draco (ed. Ziegler, 1954). Göttingen, 1939-.

II. Commentaries, Monographs and Periodical

Articles on the Gospel according to Matthew

Allen, W. C., A Critical and Exegetical Commentary on the Gospel according to St. Matthew. New York, 1925.

Barth, G., "Matthew's Understanding of the Law" in G. Bornkamm, Barth, H. J. Held, Tradition and Interpretation in Matthew. ET: Philadelphia, 1963, pp. 58-164.

181

182

Billerbeck, P., Kommentar zum Neuen Testament aus Talmud und Midrach, V. I, Das Evangelium nach Matthäus. Munich, 1922.

Blair, E. P., Jesus in the Gospel of Matthew. New York, 1960.

Bonnard, P., L'Évangile selon St. Matthieu. Paris, 1963.

Bornkamm, G., "Der Auferstandene und die Irdische, Mt. 28:16-20" in Zeit und Geschichte (Dankesgabe an R. Bultmann zum 80. Geburtstag; E. Dinkler, ed.). Tübingen, 1964, pp. 172-91.

_____, "End-Expectation and Church in Matthew" in Bornkamm, G. Barth, H. J. Held, Tradition and Interpretation in Matthew. ET: Philadelphia, 1963, pp. 15-51.

Chase, F. J., "The Lord's Command to Baptize (Mt. 28:19)." Journal of Theological Studies 6 (1905), 481-521.

Conybeare, F. C., "The Eusebian Form of the Text Mt. 28:19." ZNW 2 (1901), 275-88.

_____, "Three Early Doctrinal Modifications of the Text of the Gospels." Hibbert Journal 1 (1902), 96-113.

Cuneo, B. H., The Lord's Command to Baptize. Washington, 1923.

Davies, W. D., The Setting of the Sermon on the Mount. Cambridge, 1964.

Ellis, I. P., "But Some Doubted." NTS 14 (1967-8), 574-80.

Filson, F., The Gospel According to St. Matthew. New York, 1960.

Flusser, David, "The Conclusion of Matthew in a New Jewish Christian Source," ASTI 5 (1967), 110-20.

Gaechter, P., Das Matthäus-Evangelium. Innsbruck, 1963.

_____, Die Literarische Kunst im Matthäus-Evangelium. Stuttgart, 1966.

Grundmann, W., Das Evangelium nach Matthäus. Berlin, 1968.

Johnson, S., "Matthew, Exegesis." IB, 7.

Kilpatrick, C. D., The Origins of the Gospel According to St. Matthew. Oxford, 1946.

Kosmala, H., "The Conclusion of Matthew," ASTI 4 (1965), 132-47.

Lohmeyer, E., Das Evangelium des Matthäus. Göttingen, 1956.

Lohmeyer, E., "'Mir est gegeben alle Gewalt!'-Eine Exegese von Mt. 28:16-20." In Memorian Ernst Lohmeyer (W. Schmauch, ed.). Stuttgart, 1951, pp. 22-49.

McKenzie, J. L., "The Gospel According to Matthew." JBC, II.

McNeile, A. H., The Gospel According to St. Matthew. London, 1915.

Malina, B., "The Literary Structure and Form of Mt. 28:16-20." NTS 17 (1970), 87-103.

Michel, O., "Der Abschluss des Matthäus-Evangeliums." Ev Th 10 (1950-51), 16-26.

Schille, G., "Das Evangelium des Matthäus als Katechismus." NTS 4 (1957-8), 101-14.

Stendahl, K., "Matthew." PCB.

_____, The School of St. Matthew. Uppsala, 1954.

Strecker, G., Der Weg der Gerechtigkeit. Göttingen, 1962.

_____, "The Concept of History in Matthew." Journal of the American Academy of Religion 35 (1967), 219-30.

Trilling, W., Das Wahre Israel. Munich, 1964.[3]

III. Other Literature

Aland, K., "Der wiedergefundene Markusschluss? (Eine methodologische Bemerkung zur textkritischen Arbeit)." Z Th K 67 (1960), 3-13.

Baltzer, K., "Considerations Regarding the Office and Calling of the Prophet." HTR 61 (1968), 567-91.

Beare, F., The Earliest Records of Jesus. New York, 1962.

Blank, S., "Traces of Prophetic Agony in Isaiah." Hebrew Union College Annual 27 (1956), 81-92.

Blenkinsopp, J., "Deuteronomy." JBC, I.

Brown, R. and D. Stanley, "Aspects of New Testament Thought." JBC, II.

_____, The Gospel according to John. Anchor Bible. Vols. 29 (Jn. I-XI) and 29A (Jn. XII-XXI). Garden City, N.Y.; 1966 and 1970.

Bultmann, R., The Gospel of John. ET: Philadelphia, 1971.

184

Bultmann, R., The History of the Synoptic Tradition. ET: Oxford, 1963.

_____, Theology of the New Testament. 2 Vols. ET: Oxford, 1955.

Conzelmann, H., The Theology of St. Luke. ET: New York, 1960.

Coutourier, G., "Jeremiah." JBC, I.

Delling, G., "The Significance of the Resurrection of Jesus for Faith
    in Jesus" in book by same title (ed. C. F. D. Moule). Naperville,
    Illinois; 1968.

Dibelius, M., Die Formgeschichte des Evangeliums. Tübingen,[4] 1961.

_____, Studies in the Acts of the Apostles. ET: London, 1956.

Dillon, R. and J. Fitzmyer, "Acts of the Apostles." JBC, II.

Dodd, C. H., Historical Tradition in the Fourth Gospel. Cambridge, 1963.

____,"The Appearances of the Risen Christ: An Essay in Form-Criticism
    of the Gospels"in Studies in the Gospels (Essays in Memory of
    R. H. Lightfoot) (ed. D. E. Nineham). Oxford, 1956, pp. 9-35.

____, "The Primitive Catechism and the Sayings of Jesus" in Dodd, More
    New Testament Studies. Grand Rapids, Michigan; 1968, pp. 11-29.

Dungan, D., The Sayings of Jesus in the Churches of Paul. Philadelphia,
    1971.

Elliott, J. K., "The Text and Language of the Endings to Mark's Gospel."
    Theol Z 27 (1971), 255-62.

Ellis, E. E., The Gospel of Luke. London, 1966.

Engnell, I., The Call of Isaiah. Uppsala, 1949.

Eissfeldt, O., The Old Testament: An Introduction. ET: Oxford, 1965.

Evans, C. F., Resurrection and the New Testament. Naperville, Ill.; 1970.

Fiedler, P., Die Formel "Und Siehe" im Neuen Testament. Munich, 1969.

Fitzmyer, J., "The Letter to the Galatians." JBC, II.

_____, and R. Dillon, "Acts of the Apostles." JBC, II.

Flender, H., St. Luke: Theologian of Redemptive History. ET: New
    York, 1967.

Frankfort, H., Kingship and the Gods. Chicago, 1948.

Fuller, R., The Formation of the Resurrection Narratives. New York, 1971.

Grant, F. C., "Mark, Exegesis." IB, 7.

Greeven, H., "Προσκυνέω." TDNT, VI.

Grundmann, W., Das Evangelium nach Lukas. Berlin, 1961.

_____, Das Evangelium nach Markus. Berlin, 1962.

Habel, N., "The Form and Significance of the Call Narratives." ZAW Band 77, Heft 3 (1965) 297-323.

Hahn, F., Mission in the New Testament. ET: Naperville, Ill.; 1965.

Hertzberg, H., I and II Samuel. ET: Philadelphia, 1964.

Huesman, J., "Exodus." JBC, I.

Hyatt, J. P., "Jeremiah, Exegesis." IB, 5.

Jeremias, J., Jesus' Promise to the Nations. ET: Naperville, Ill.; 1958.

Käsemann, E., The Testament of Jesus. ET: London, 1968.

Kaster, J., The Literature and Mythology of Ancient Egypt. London, 1968.

Köster, H., Synoptische Überlieferung bei den Apostolischen Vätern. Berlin, 1957.

Kümmel, W., Introduction to the New Testament. ET: New York, 1966.

Kuntz, J. K., The Self-Revelation of God. Philadelphia, 1967.

Lampe, G. W. H., "Luke." PCB.

Lebreton, J., Histoire du Dogme de la Trinité des Origines à St. Augustin, V. 1, Les Origines. Paris, 1919.

Lindblom, J., Prophecy in Ancient Israel. ET: New York, 1965.

Linnemann, E., "Der (wiedergefundene) Markusschluss." Z Th K 66 (1969), 255-87.

Lohfink, N., Die deuteronomistische Darstellung des Übergangs der Führung Israels von Moses auf Josue. Scholastik 37 (1962), 32-44.

Maly, E., "Genesis." JBC, I.

Marxsen, W., The Resurrection of Jesus of Nazareth. ET: Philadelphia, 1970.

Mauchline, J., "1-2 Kings." PCB.

Menoud, P.,"Remarques sur les textes de l'Ascension dans Luc-Actes," in Neutestamentliche Studien für R. Bultmann (ed. W. Eltester). Berlin, 1954, pp. 148-56.

Meye, R., "The Ending of Mark's Gospel." B Res 14 (1969), 33-43.

Myers, J., Ezra-Nehemiah, Anchor Bible. V. 14. Garden City, New York; 1965.

Muilenburg, J., "Ezekiel." PCB.

_____, "Form Criticism and Beyond." JBL 88 (1969), 1-18.

Munck, J., Paul and the Salvation of Mankind. ET: Richmond, Va.; 1959.

_____,"Discours d'adieu dans le Nouveau Testament et dans la littérature biblique," in Aux Sources de la Tradition Chrétienne (Melanges Goguel). Paris, 1950, pp. 155-70.

Neirynck, F., "Les Femmes au Tombeau." NTS 15 (1969), 168-90.

North, R., "The Chronicler: 1-2 Chronicles, Ezra, Nehemiah." JBC, I.

Noth, M., Exodus. ET: Philadelphia, 1962.

Ogg, G., "Chronology of the New Testament." PCB.

Paterson, J., "Jeremiah." PCB.

Pines, S., "The Jewish Christians of the First Century according to a New Source." Proceedings of the Israeli Academy of Sciences and Humanities II (Jerusalem, 1968), pp. 237-310.

Quasten, J., Patrology, V. I, The Beginnings of Patristic Literature. Westminster, Md.; 1962.

Rad, G. von, Deuteronomy. ET: Philadelphia, 1966.

___, Genesis. ET: Philadelphia, 1961.

___, Old Testament Theology, V. II. ET: New York, 1965.

Roberts, B. J., "The Canon and Text of the Old Testament." <u>PCB</u>.

Rohde, J., Rediscovering the Teaching of the Evangelists. ET: Philadelphia, 1968.

Schmid, J., Das Evangelium nach Lukas. Regensburg, 1960.

Schmidt, K. L., "Ἔθνος in the New Testament." <u>TDNT</u>, II.

Schofield, J. N., "Judges." <u>PCB</u>.

Schweizer, E., "Πνεῦμα, Πνευματικός." <u>TDNT</u>, VI.

Speiser, E., Genesis, Anchor Bible, V. I. Garden City, N.Y.; 1964.

Stampvoort, P. A. von, "The Interpretation of the Ascension in Luke and Acts." <u>NTS</u> 5 (1958), 30-42.

Stalker, D., "Exodus." <u>PCB</u>.

Stuhmueller, C., "The Gospel According to Luke." <u>JBC</u>, II.

Stanley, D. and R. Brown, "Aspects of New Testament Thought." <u>JBC</u>, II.

Swete, H. B., The Gospel According to St. Mark. New York, 1898.

Taylor, V., The Gospel According to St. Mark. New York, 1966.[2]

Tödt, H., The Son of Man in the Synoptic Tradition. ET: Philadelphia, 1965.

Vawter, B., "The Gospel According to John." <u>JBC</u>, II.

Westermann, C., Isaiah 40-60. ET: Philadelphia, 1969.

Wickenhauser, A., New Testament Introduction. ET: New York, 1958.

Wilder, A., "Variant Traditions of the Resurrection in Acts." <u>JBL</u> 62 (1943), 306-11.

Wilson, R. McL., "Mark." <u>PCB</u>.

Zimmerli, W., Ezechiel. Neukirchen, The Netherlands; 1969.

HIEBERT LIBRARY

3 6877 00100 3861